Shooter in a Worked World: John Pesek and the 1920s Promotional Wars

By Ken Zimmerman Jr.

Shooter in a Worked World: John Pesek and the 1920s Promotional Wars

Copyright 2024 by Ken Zimmerman Jr.

Published by Ken Zimmerman Jr. Enterprises www.kenzimmermanjr.com

All rights reserved. No portion of this book may be reproduced, stored in a retrieval system, or transmitted in any form or by any means—electronic, mechanical, photocopy, recording, or any other—except for brief quotations in printed reviews without the prior permission of the publisher.

Published in St. Louis, Missouri by Ken Zimmerman Jr. Enterprises.

First Edition: September 2024

If you like this book, you can sign up for Ken's newsletter to receive information about future book releases. You can sign up for the newsletter and receive an added e-book at kenzimmermanjr.com.

Table of Contents

Introduction 6

Chapter 1 – Early Exploits 10

Chapter 2 – Early Big Matches 20

Chapter 3 – Plestina Struggles for Bookings 44

Chapter 4 – Busting the Trust Buster 70

Chapter 5 – Curley's New Challenger 88

Chapter 6 – Pesek and Pendleton Before the Big Match 105

Chapter 7 – Upsetting an Olympic Champion and Jack Curley 125

Chapter 8 – Life Before the Double-Cross 138

Chapter 9 – A Fateful Decision 154

Chapter 10 – The 1926 Series of Matches with Joe Stecher 166

Chapter 11 – Champion Dog Breeder 177

Conclusion 187

Other Combat Sports Books by Ken Zimmerman Jr. 193

Bibliography 194

About the Author 200

Endnotes 202

Introduction

John "Tigerman" Pesek occupies a unique place in American professional wrestling history. Also known as "The Nebraska Tigerman," Pesek debuted in the professional ring in 1914. Although professional wrestlers worked their matches by this time, Pesek was a skilled "hooker" or submission wrestler. Pesek could legitimately defeat his opponents.

Pesek's skill and open disdain for the "worked" nature of professional wrestling made promoters wary of booking him. The promoters did not want Pesek to double-cross them by defeating the stars that promoters brought Pesek in to make look good.

Promoters did find an effective use for Pesek's skills in the early 1920s. A series of promotional wars caused rival promoters to recruit legitimate wrestlers to wrestle for them and challenge the reigning champion. While insiders considered Ed "Strangler" Lewis equal to the task, the promoters controlling the World Heavyweight Wrestling Championship were hesitant to make the match.

The promoters decided it would be better to match Pesek with these "trustbusters." If the wrestler, like Marin Plestina, defeated Pesek, Lewis agreed to wrestle a contest with Plestina. The trust promoters figured even if the other wrestler won, Pesek would hurt the trust buster badly. The promoter could then force the injured wrestler to wrestle Lewis before the challenger healed up making it even harder for the challenger to defeat Lewis.

Pesek was happy to wrestle for the promoters in these ventures. First, the trust promoters paid Pesek an enormous amount to wrestle and hurt the challenger. Second, the promoters and opponents knew that the matches would be "shoots" or legitimate contests. Pesek could not wait to wrestle the decorated wrestlers in legitimate matches.

Pesek's first challenge would be Marin Plestina, five feet, eleven inch, 240-pound monster, who Martin "Farmer" Burns trained for professional wrestling. 34-year-old Plestina had the advantage in size and experience. Would it be enough?

Figure 1- John "The Nebraska Tigerman" Pesek (Public Domain)

Chapter 1 – Early Exploits

Before we examine the Pesek vs. Plestina match, we need to look at the early career of John "The Nebraska Tigerman" Pesek. Why did the promoters choose Pesek out of all the shooters and hookers available to settle high-profile promotional contests.

Pesek began his career quietly enough in his home state of Nebraska. Pesek was born in Ravenna, Nebraska on February 2, 1894. Pesek wrestled locally before turning professional in 1914.

Pesek wrestled in Nebraska for the first three years of his career because Pesek helped his brothers on their father's family farm. Pesek eventually led two brothers and his son, Jack, Jr., into the professional wrestling ranks.

Pesek wrestled professionally for about a year before I find the first reference to one of his matches in August 1915. On Saturday, August 7, 1915, Pesek wrestled Young Dean, a wrestler from Ohio. Young Dean claimed to be undefeated.[i]

Pesek defeated Young Dean in two straight falls in under five minutes. The Grand Island Independent opined "…if it is a fact that Dean has never been defeated it is a cinch that he has either not wrestled at all or has been taking on poor talent."[ii]

In September 1915, Pesek wrestled his mentor and trainer, Clarence Ecklund, a light heavyweight wrestler at the Ravenna, Nebraska fire department's annual picnic. Pesek and Ecklund worked an exhibition for an hour or more before Pesek conceded the match to Ecklund due to exhaustion.[iii]

On Saturday, October 30, 1915, Pesek wrestled another well-thought of Nebraska wrestler, John Foreman. Pesek wrestled Foreman to prove to promoters, fans, and newspaper reporters who the next up-and-coming wrestler from Nebraska would be.

Figure 2 - Clarence Ecklund, who mentored and trained John Pesek (Public Domain)

Pesek and Foreman wrestled at the Hostetler Opera House. The men wrestled a best two-out-of-three-falls match.

Pesek used a scissors hold to pin Foreman in two minutes, thirty seconds for the first fall.[iv] Pesek rushed matters in the first fall.

Pesek calmed down during the second fall. Pesek pinned Foreman for the second fall in eight minutes, ten seconds. Pesek dominated the match winning in two straight falls. Pesek showed he would be the top young grappler.

On Tuesday, November 23, 1915, Pesek wrestled local baseball player Joe Bills. Pesek took on Bills at the Hostetler Opera House in Shelton, Nebraska. The men wrestled a two-out-of-three-falls match.

Martin "Farmer" Burns trained Bills for wrestling. Bills showed this training in the first fall. Bills surprised Pesek with a quick pin in one minute for the first fall. Pesek did not make the same mistake again.

Pesek used the leg scissors to pin Bills for the next two falls. It took Pesek five minutes to secure the second fall. Pesek needed another five minutes to take the third fall and match after the brief scare.[v]

Either Charley or Hubert Pesek, Pesek's younger brothers, wrestled a thirty-minute draw on the undercard. Both men wrestled briefly before returning to full-time farming.

In building up the young John Pesek, The *Ravenna News* carried a story about Pesek's feats of strength. The newspaper story claimed that Pesek could bust a bag of wheat or crush a gallon water jug by squeezing each object with a leg scissors.[vi] Managers occasionally paid newspaper reporters to author such stories but local newspaper reporters often authored favorable articles about local celebrities.

Pesek suffered his first setback in December 1915. Jake Amens won the first and third falls from Pesek in Ravenna.

Pesek took the second fall. The coverage claimed Pesek was still an amateur giving the professionals a tough time.[vii]

Figure 3- Charles Pesek circa 1919 (Public Domain)

In February 1916, Pesek took a break from the ring to have a minor operation on his ear. Pesek did not say whether wrestling caused the injury.

At the end of April 1916, Charles Pesek threw John Herzog at the Gibbon, Nebraska Opera House. Charles Pesek wrestled John Pesek in an exhibition match after defeating Herzog.

On Saturday, May 6, 1916, John Pesek wrestled his first match since losing to Jake Amens. Pesek wrestled Amens at the Hostetler Opera House in Shelton, Nebraska.

Pesek got revenge on Jake Amens and won a $200 purse. Amens agreed to throw Pesek twice in an hour. Amens did not throw Pesek once.[viii] Pesek's brother Charley also won a $50 purse by defeating his opponent.

On Tuesday, May 23, 1916, Pesek wrestled John Lenz of Fremont, Nebraska at the Hostetler Opera House in Shelton, Nebraska. Pesek defeated Lenz in two straight falls.

Pesek won the first fall in three minutes, three seconds with a leg scissors. Pesek won the second fall and match in one minute, fifty-three seconds with another leg scissors.[ix] Pesek's younger brothers Charles and Hubert wrestled an exhibition before Pesek wrestled Lenz.

Pesek toured Nebraska in June 1916 defeating all the local wrestlers. Pesek suffered a soft tissue injury to his knee and ankle throwing one of the local wrestlers. Pesek was inactive for weeks while he recovered from the injury.

At the end of July 1916, lightning struck a garage on the farm of John Pesek's mother. The lightning caused a fire, which burned up John Pesek's brand new $1,250 Reo car.[x]

In 2024 dollars, the car would be worth $30,120.00. Pesek smartly insured the car.

John Pesek wrestled George Kinney in Cairo, Nebraska on Saturday, August 26,

1916. Pesek defeated Kinney in two straight falls.

On Thursday, September 14, 1916, Pesek wrestled Chris Jordan in a match between Nebraska's top wrestlers. Four hundred fans filled the Hostetler Opera House to watch the heralded match. Pesek and Jordan wrestled to an inconclusive two-hour draw.[xi]

Fans booed the referee, who fans felt favored Jordon throughout the contest. Pesek showed in his first two years that it would take an exceptional wrestler to beat him. Pesek did not know at the time that these early battles were preparing him for the promotional wars of the 1920s.

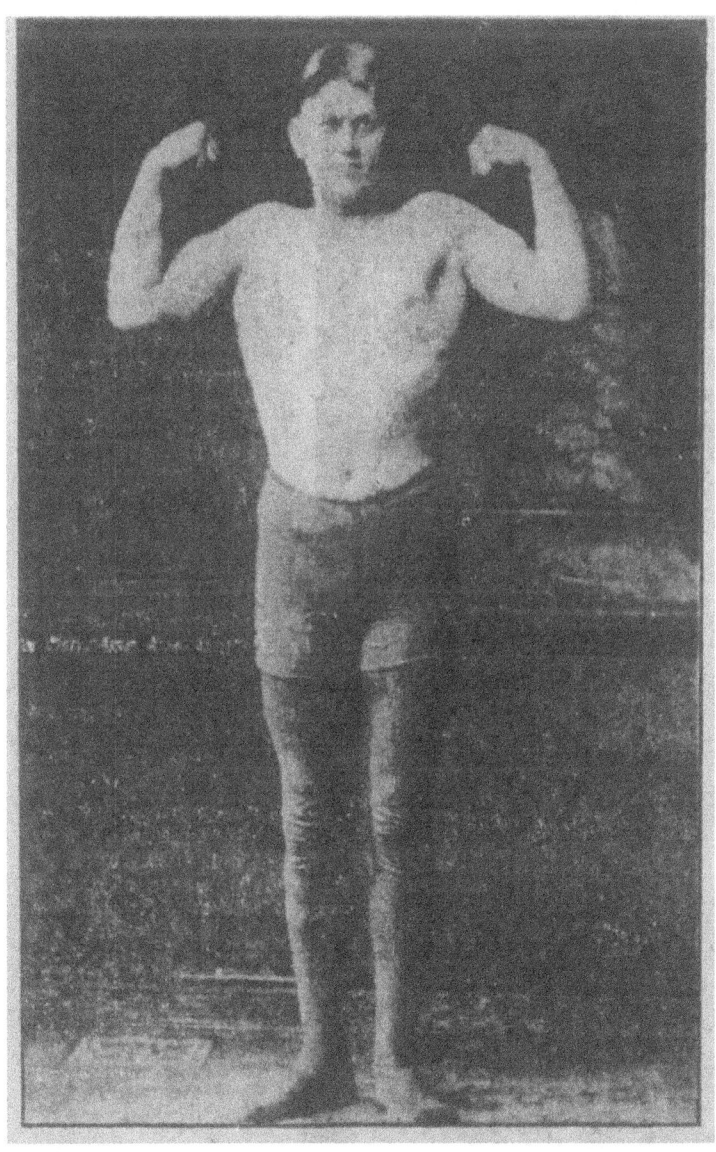

Figure 4 - John Pesek circa 1916 (Public Domain)

Chapter 2 – Early Big Matches

On Tuesday, December 12, 1916, John Pesek wrestled Al Mantell at the Hostetler Opera House in Shelton, Nebraska. I included this match on Pesek's early big matches to clear up confusion not because it was a big match.

If Al Mantell were the original "Dutch Mantell," Alfred Albert Joseph de Real Gardiur, it would be a big match. "Dutch Mantell" was one of the greatest shooters and hookers of all-time.

The picture of Al Mantell in the advertisements leading into the match show this wrestler is too young to be Dutch Mantell. The original Dutch Mantell looked like he fell out of the top of the ugly tree and hit every branch on the way down.

Pesek pinned Mantell in two straight falls in under twenty-four minutes also proving that Pesek did not wrestle the original Dutch Mantell.[xii] Pesek did wrestle big names though.

Figure 5 - Al Mantell, who I do not believe is the original Dutch Mantell (Public Domain)

On Thursday, January 18, 1917, Pesek wrestled future World Champion Earl

Caddock in a handicapped stipulations match. Caddock agreed to throw Pesek twice in one hour or concede the match to Pesek.

Caddock won the World Heavyweight Wrestling Championship from Joe Stecher in what may have been a contest during April 1917. Obviously, Pesek was not on Caddock's level yet, so Caddock agreed to throw Pesek twice in an hour to even things up competitively.

Pesek wrestled Caddock in front of a packed Hostetler Opera House in Minden, Nebraska. Builders erected the Opera House, which still stands as the W. T. Thorne Building, in 1891.

The men wrestled in a ring, which was becoming more common in professional wrestling. During the 1910s, professional wrestling promoters transitioned from wrestlers wrestling on mats or carpet on a stage to the wrestlers wrestling in rings like professional boxers.

The fans watched a boring contest. Each time Caddock threatened to take Pesek down, Pesek escaped to the ropes causing the referee to break the men and return them to a standing position in the middle of the ring. Using these tactics, Pesek prevented Caddock from throwing him once during the sixty minutes.

Pesek did take Caddock down twice, which surprised both Caddock and the fans. Caddock's supporters, who travelled from Iowa to watch the match, left disappointed. The Caddock supporters bet heavily on their favorite and were surprised by the skills of the newcomer. Pesek cost the Caddock supporters a hefty sum of money which had never happened before.[xiii]

Caddock wanted to avenge this loss and expressed a desire to wrestle Pesek in a finish match. Pesek agreed but before promoters and managers arranged a rematch, Caddock defeated Stecher for the world title. Between World War I and

Caddock's early retirement, Caddock only wrestled Pesek once more in late 1920.[xiv]

On Friday, February 9, 1917, Pesek wrestled future promotional war opponent Marin Plestina on the undercard of Joe Stecher's title defense against Charlie Peters. Pesek wrestled Plestina to a twenty-minute draw.[xv]

Pesek operated out of Nebraska at the beginning of his wrestling career which did not hurt him as much as it normally would because World Champion Joe Stecher often wrestled in his home state of Nebraska as well. Stecher's preference for wrestling big matches in Omaha, Nebraska kept a steady stream of nationally known wrestlers travelling to Nebraska.

In April 1917, Pesek wrestled his first match with Jim Londos, the biggest box office draw of the 1930s and professional wrestling in general. In 1917, Londos had just started wrestling professionally outside the carnivals.

Figure 6 - Jim Londos circa 1920 (Public Domain)

Londos started his career as a carnival strongman. The carnival wrestlers taught Londos how to shoot and hook. Londos developed into a competent although not great hooker.

On Thursday, April 4, 1917, Pesek wrestled Londos at the Hostetler Opera House in Minden, Nebraska. The match ended controversially when the referee Evan Smith disqualified Londos for using a strangle hold on Pesek.

The first controversy occurred before the match started when Pesek's manager, Martin Slattery, objected to the out-of-town referee. Slattery insisted on a local referee.

Chris Jordan, who served as Londos' manager, urged Londos to call off the match. Instead, Londos accepted local referee Evan Smith.[xvi]

According to the *Omaha Daily Bee*, the Londos supporters lost over $2,000.00 in bets. With the odd switch of the referee, controversial ending, and large gambling losses, this match may be the first match Pesek worked with his opponent.

Figure 7 - Bob Managoff, Sr. around 1921 (Public Domain)

After the Londos match, Pesek wrestled local wrestlers until he met

Bobby Managoff, Sr. at the Nebraska State Fair in Greeley, Nebraska on Thursday, September 20, 1917. Pesek defeated Managoff in two straight falls.

Pesek won the first fall in fifteen minutes, sixteen seconds with a body scissors and arm bar. Pesek won the second fall and match with a head scissors and wrist lock in five minutes, twenty seconds.[xvii]

Pesek's dominant defeat of Managoff is particularly impressive because Managoff was a nationally known world title contender. Frank Gotch was wrestling Bob Managoff in a training match in 1915 when Gotch broke his lower leg killing the Frank Gotch versus Joe Stecher title match in the summer of 1915.

At the end of October 1917, Pesek suffered the same fate as Gotch. Pesek was training for a match with Jack Taylor when Pesek broke two bones near his ankle.[xviii] The injury left Pesek inactive to end 1917.

After recovering from the injury and dealing with a couple of cancellations by Taylor, Pesek finally wrestled Taylor at the Liederkranz Auditorium in Grand Island, Nebraska on Friday, March 29, 1918. Pesek's earlier injury almost cost Pesek the match.

Pesek won the first fall in twenty-one minutes with a body scissors and arm lock. During the pinfall, Pesek reinjured the ankle. Pesek wrestled defensively for the rest of the match as Pesek could not put weight on his injured leg.[xix]

Taylor could not take advantage of Pesek's compromised condition stalemating the match for almost two hours. The defensive posturing for two hours bored the one thousand fans who crowded the Liederkranz Auditorium. After two hours and twenty minutes, the referee awarded the match to Pesek for taking the only fall.

JACK TAYLOR.
Former heavyweight wrestling champion of Canada, who is to clash with John Pesek, the Shelton cyclone, Wednesday night, March 27, at the Lincoln auditorium.

Figure 8 - Jack Taylor circa 1918 (Public Domain)

Pesek spent the rest of the summer trying to get a match with Caddock, Stecher, Zbyszko, or Ed "Strangler" Lewis. However, Caddock joining the Army and Stecher joining the Navy made setting up these matches difficult. Zbyszko did not seem too eager to wrestle Pesek.

In October 1918, the U.S. Army drafted Pesek and his manager Martin Slattery ending Pesek's 1918 campaign.[xx] Circumstances forced Pesek to wait until 1919 to see if promoters would book Pesek in a match against the "Big Four" or if promoters would freeze Pesek out like Marin Plestina.

World War I disturbingly affected the Pesek family, when the U.S. Army notified the family that Hubert Pesek, Charley's twin brother, died in France. A soldier in his outfit reported that shrapnel struck Hubert Pesek in the unoccupied zone between the German and American trenches on October 11, 1918. Hubert Pesek collapsed on the ground.

The soldier saw medics pick up the lifeless body of Hubert Pesek and remove him from the field. The Army could not find Hubert Pesek but believed the report of his death.

Hubert Pesek joined the U.S. Army on August 25, 1917. Pesek shipped out with the American Expeditionary Force to France in early 1918. Prior to his death, Hubert Pesek went over the top of the trench fifteen times to engage the enemy in the unoccupied zone between the trenches.[xxi]

The family mourned Hubert's desk until March 1919. John Pesek was wrestling in Omaha, when a soldier, who recently came home to Brainard, Nebraska, told John Pesek that he saw "Curley" Pesek, Hubert's nickname, in a French hospital.[xxii]

Despite John Pesek's assertion that the Germans could not kill "Curley" with one bullet, John Pesek expressed skepticism. However, events proved the Brainard soldier correct.

The War Department sent the Pesek family a telegram saying Hubert Pesek landed in Newport News, Virginia, from France in April 1919. The U.S. Army did not know Hubert Pesek was in a French hospital recovering from his injuries. Having lost track of Hubert, the War Department sent the family a notice of death based on the field report from Hubert Pesek's last battle.[xxiii]

When Hubert returned home, John Pesek realized Hubert's wrestling career was over. The German's had gassed Hubert, who was still weak after recovering for six months.[xxiv] Hubert helped John and Charley Pesek on John Pesek's farm until Hubert married. Hubert bought his own farm and started commercial farming.

After the worry over Hubert, John Pesek learned of an opportunity to break in against the Big Four. World War I made wrestling promoters, who struggled to hold cards since most wrestlers served in the United States military in one fashion or another, desperate to make money. A

Nebraska Stockmen's Association Convention provided one of wrestling's greediest promoters an opportunity to make a good payday.

Figure 9 - Wladek Zbyszko (Public Domain)

The Stockmen's Association staged their convention in tiny Gordon, Nebraska with a population of around one thousand five hundred residents. The convention temporarily boosted the town's population to eight to ten thousand. Jack Curley, the New York promoter, decided to bring Wladek Zbyszko to Nebraska for a match with John Pesek.

Curley's gambit paid off financially, but it set Zbyszko back as a contender. Four to five thousand fans crowded into the outdoor venue to watch local favorite Pesek wrestle nationally known Zbyszko on June 14, 1919. Promoters filled the ringside seats, which the promoters sold for ten dollars.[xxv] Between the gate and the gambling, the promoters and wrestlers took home a large payday from the match.

Like other contests, Pesek did not wrestle the most action-packed match with Wladek Zbyszko. The men traded positions for the first hour before Pesek got behind Zbyszko. Pesek maintained back control for the next hour.

After an hour of Pesek working Zbyszko over, Zbyszko stood back to his feet. Pesek lifted Zbyszko in the air with a waist hold dumping Zbyszko back to the mat.

Going in for the kill, Pesek applied a head scissors on the exhausted Zbyszko. Pesek combined the head scissors with a wrist lock to pin Zbyszko for the first and only fall in two hours, three minutes, and fifteen seconds.[xxvi] The referee declared Pesek the winner. Neither Curley nor Zbyszko protested the decision.

Pesek cleanly pinned Zbyszko to establish Pesek on the national stage. With a victory over both Caddock and Wladek Zbyszko, fans and newspaper reporters looked at Pesek as a world championship contender.

In August 1919, Joe Stecher backed out of a proposed match with Pesek at the Nebraska State Fair in September. Pesek even agreed to give Stecher all the receipts from the gate of what would have been a huge payday if Pesek could not defeat Stecher. Stecher refused to sign the agreement.[xxvii]

Unable to secure a match with Stecher, Pesek instead wrestled Jim

Londos in Omaha, Nebraska on October 10, 1919. Londos was not a member of the "Big Four," but Londos had built a national reputation. Promoters recognized Londos drawing power as a potential top star.

The national wrestling trust led by Jack Curley promised Pesek and his manager Martin Slattery that Pesek could wrestle one of the "Big Four" if Pesek defeated Londos.[xxviii] Pesek had his doubts after the earlier disappointments.

Pesek fouled Marin Plestina continuously with slaps and palm strikes in their 1921 match. In this match, Londos played the Pesek role by slapping and palm striking Pesek. Londos pushed Pesek off the stage into the spectators once or twice. The referee warned Londos repeatedly but never disqualified Londos.

An angry Pesek applied a toe hold which looked to finish Londos. Londos rolled wildly to relieve the pressure of the hold. After thrashing about for a minute, Londos freed himself and stood back to his feet.

Londos used a grapevine and half-Nelson to take Pesek to the mat. Londos and his seconds claimed a fall. However, the referee, Kid Graves, the Sporting Editor for the *Omaha Daily Bee* said Londos did not score a pinfall.[xxix]

Pesek pinned Londos' arms to his side, lifted Londos into the air, and slammed Londos to the ground. Pesek followed Londos to the ground. The force of the slam and Pesek falling on Londos knocked Londos out. Graves awarded Pesek the first fall at two hours, twenty-six minutes, and thirty seconds.[xxx]

After the fifteen-minute intermission, Londos returned to the mat and wrestled for about a minute. After Londos visibly staggered, his corner threw in a towel signifying Londos conceded the match to Pesek.

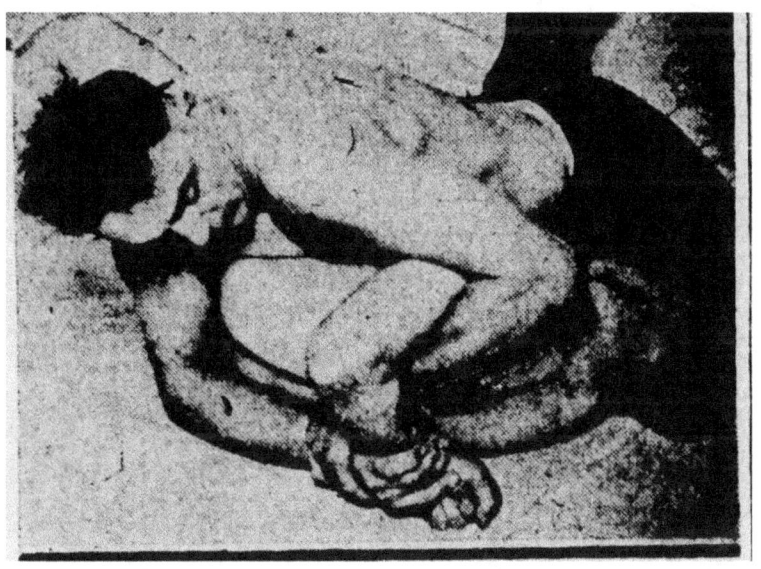

Figure 10- Joe Stecher showing the double-arm wristlock on his brother Anton "Tony" Stecher (Public Domain)

Now it was time to see if Curley would live up to his word. Mat observers excused Pesek for being skeptical that Curley would follow through on his promise based on Curley's corrupt reputation. However, Curley finally delivered. Curley matched Pesek against Joe Stecher in Omaha, Nebraska on January 16, 1920.

Six thousand fans crowded into Omaha's Auditorium to watch the two Nebraska wrestlers meet for the first time.^{xxxi} It took over two years to book the match, but the highly expected match was a huge payday for the promoters, managers, and wrestlers.

Pesek and Stecher traded positions for the first two hours without either man securing an advantage. Stecher applied two or three leg scissors to the body. Pesek escaped each attempt.

After two hours of even wrestling, Stecher secured a fourth body scissors. This time Stecher also applied a double-arm wristlock. Pesek verbally gave up the fall rather than suffer a serious shoulder injury.^{xxxii} Stecher took the first fall in two hours, three minutes.

Pesek was out for revenge in the second fall. Pesek slammed Stecher two or three times before securing a body scissors and wristlock to pin Stecher in thirteen minutes to even the match up at one fall apiece.

The third fall provided the biggest surprise of the evening. Pesek had Stecher's back with his legs wrapped around Stecher's waist. Stecher was stuck in the worst position for a wrestler or grappler.

Stecher reached back and wrapped his arms around Pesek's head while pulling Pesek's head forward. Stecher pushed with his feet to put all his weight on Pesek's chest forcing Pesek's shoulders to the mat for the third fall and match.[xxxiii]

Stecher's move was either a brilliant in-ring improvisation or evidence that Stecher and Pesek worked the match. Neither sport reporters nor fans had ever seen the move.

After the match with Stecher, Pesek wrestled outside of Nebraska for the first time during the year of 1920. Pesek worked the family farm in Ravenna, Nebraska with his brothers, so Pesek did not like to be far from home. Pesek realized that he would never be a world title contender if he did not leave home for big matches.

On December 28, 1920, Pesek travelled to Des Moines, Iowa to wrestle former World Heavyweight Wrestling Champion Earl Caddock. Pesek defeated Caddock in a handicapped match in 1917.

In this match, Caddock wrestled Pesek at the Coliseum in Des Moines. Caddock only wrestled two more years before retiring. At the time of this match, Caddock was still one of the top professional wrestlers in the United States.

Caddock wrestled carefully. Pesek wrestled defensively. For the first forty minutes, Caddock and Pesek provided little action for the fans.

Finally, Caddock worked a wristlock and half-Nelson combination before applying a hammerlock. Caddock forced Pesek to give up to the hammerlock at one hour, eight minutes, and twenty seconds.[xxxiv]

Caddock looked exhausted but Pesek entered the second fall clearly favoring the arm that Caddock hammer locked. Caddock needed only seven minutes to win the match in straight falls with another hammerlock.ˣˣˣᵛ

As events in 1921 would prove, Curley made peace with Pesek and Slattery just in time. Curley would enlist Pesek to end Curley's high profile promotional war with former promotional partner, Tex Rickard.

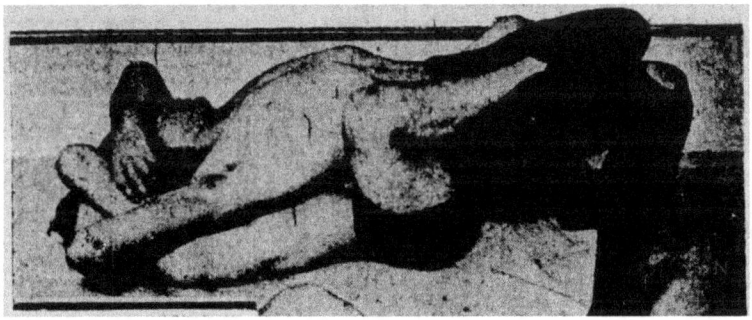

Figure 11 -Joe Stecher shows the pin Stecher executed on Pesek. Anton "Tony" Stecher is helping his brother Joe show the pin. (Public Domain)

Chapter 3 – Plestina Struggles for Bookings

Plestina's angst with the dominant promoters stemmed from a match in September 1917 against former World Heavyweight Wrestling Champion Joe Stecher. Plestina wrestled Stecher on Labor Day, Monday, September 3rd in Omaha, Nebraska. At the time, Plestina wrestled out of Omaha, while Stecher lived in nearby Dodge, Nebraska.

Wrestlers worked most matches in this era. However, Stecher and Plestina wrestled a contest in this match.

Plestina convinced himself that he could defeat any professional wrestler in a legitimate contest. Martin "Farmer" Burns taught catch wrestling to Plestina, a legitimate shooter and hooker. Stecher, a shooter and hooker himself, entered the match knowing it was a legitimate contest.

Organizers feared the legitimate contest would bore fans with a long, inconclusive, and boring match. The organizers asked both camps to agree that if the referee thought one wrestler stalled throughout the contest the referee could order one wrestler to take the down position like in amateur wrestling.

Martin "Farmer" Burns agreed for Plestina while Anton "Tony" Stecher, Joe's older brother and manager, agreed for Stecher. The agreement led to a controversial ending and near riot.[xxxvi]

During the match, Plestina had an upper body strength advantage, while Stecher had the lower body strength advantage. Plestina needed to avoid Stecher's leg scissors at all costs.

Stecher and Plestina wrestled in front of a crowd of soldiers training for World War I in Omaha as well as the regular wrestling crowd. The crowd looked forward to an entertaining wrestling match, but Stecher and Plestina disappointed them.

Joe Stecher		Marin Plestina
6 ft. 1 in.	height	5 ft. 11 in.
205 pounds	weight	215 pounds
78¾ in.	reach	74 in.
16½ in.	neck	19 in.
41½ in.	chest normal	44 in.
46 in.	chest expanded	48 in.
33½ in.	waist	36 in.
13¾ in.	forearm	14 in.
26½ in.	thigh	28 in.
19½ in.	calf	17 in.
15½ in.	upper arm	17 in.
11¼ in.	ankle	10½ in.
24	age	28

Figure 12 - Stecher vs. Plestina Tale of the Tape

Stecher tried taking Plestina down repeatedly. Plestina sprawled and pushed Stecher away each time. Plestina did not try any offensive moves or holds. Plestina only concerned himself with defensive wrestling by avoiding Stecher's offense.

After two hours of Plestina's avoiding the match and a continuous chorus of boos from the fans, the referee, Edward Beets of Hooper,

Nebraska, ordered Plestina to take the down position.

Plestina refused to take the down position complaining that Stecher stalled as much as Plestina did. Beets disagreed with Plestina's assertions and demanded that Plestina take the down position.

After Plestina refused two more times to take the down position, Reets slapped Stecher on the back signifying that Stecher won the fall. When Plestina saw Reets award the fall to Stecher, Plestina punched Reets.[xxxvii]

Omaha Police Officers swarmed into the ring and pushed Plestina back to his corner. It took the police officers five minutes to control both the wrestlers and the crowd. Fortunately for the police, the soldiers surrounded the ring refusing to let any fans past them.[xxxviii] Their quick action prevented a riot.

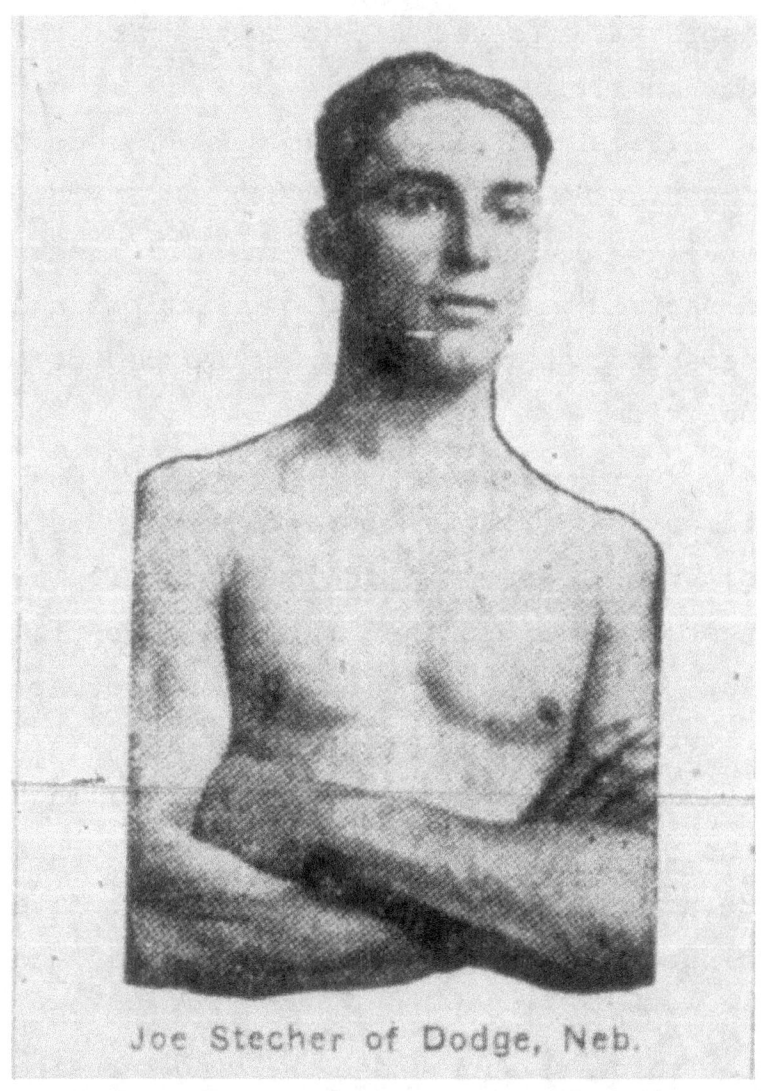

Figure 13 - Joe Stecher circa 1917 (Public Domain)

After the officials restored order, Reets ordered the match restarted. Plestina refused to report to center ring unless Reets reversed his decision and restarted the first fall.

Reets told Plestina that he disqualified Plestina for not following the agreed upon pre-match stipulations. Reets told Plestina to report to center ring for the second fall. If Plestina did not report to center ring, Reets would award the match to Stecher on Plestina's implied withdrawal.[xxxix]

Plestina stood in his corner with his arms crossed. Reets awarded the deadly dull match to Stecher.

Upon the announcement that Stecher won the match in two straight falls, Plestina charged at Reets. Omaha Police expected problems after the first fall and intervened before Plestina hit Reets again.

Plestina tried charging Reets one more time, but the Omaha Police Officers stopped him. Tiring of Plestina's actions, the Omaha Police Officers told Plestina to leave the ring, or the officers would arrest him.

The Sixth Regiment Commander had the soldiers escort the referee and wrestlers from ringside to the dressing rooms to prevent angry fans from attacking them. Plestina bore a grudge with the trust promoters, who Plestina felt purposely cheated him out of the match to diminish his status as a world title contender.

After Plestina's September 1917 match with Joe Stecher, Plestina struggled to find bookings with any of the "Big Four". In fact, Plestina struggled to find bookings with any opponents.

Plestina did not help his case by traveling to Detroit, Michigan to challenge Ed "Strangler" Lewis. Lewis's manager Billy Sandow booked Lewis out of Detroit in 1917. Plestina boldly entered the lion's den to challenge one of the "Big Four."

While in Chicago, Plestina did secure one match. On Tuesday, October 30, 1917, Plestina wrestled Paul Martinson. While Plestina did not work with

Martinson, Plestina allowed Martinson to try to apply a couple of holds before pinning Martinson with a head scissors in twenty-one minutes of the first fall.[xl]

Plestina did not extend any professional courtesy in the second fall. Plestina used a head scissors to take the second fall and match in seven minutes.[xli]

J.C. Marsh, Plestina's manager, carried a controversial reputation even for professional wrestling. Also known as Ole Marsh and Joe Carroll, Marsh served a 14-month sentence in 1910 for his involvement in a gambling ring.

John C. Mabry, a Kansas City cattle dealer, ran a gambling ring in New Orleans, the state of Colorado, and Council Bluffs, Iowa. Mabry used insiders in professional wrestling, professional boxing, and professional horse racing to steer victims into the scheme.

The operators told the victims about a fixed wrestling match, boxing bout, or horse race, and the victims bet $2,000 to

$37,000 on the outcome.[xlii] $37,000 is over a million dollars in 2024 dollars.

Despite the insider's assurance of a sure thing, an unforeseen circumstance arose that caused the victim to lose the bet. Mabry and the ring saw the circumstances fine. It was only the victim who did not see the double-cross coming.

Unfortunately for Mabry, he and his confederates used the United States mail to send instructions to the victims. Mabry unwittingly committed a federal offense by using the mail to defraud the gamblers. This mistake led to a rare prosecution of the gambling ring and prison sentences for over twenty accomplices.[xliii]

Ole Marsh steered a couple of victims to Mabry's ring. Marsh pled guilty. The court showed leniency by sentencing Marsh to 14 months in prison and fining him $1,500. The court sentenced Mabry and other defendants to 10 years in prison and $10,000 fines.[xliv]

This sentence dogged Marsh for years. Newspaper reporters brought it up any time they authored an article about the seamy side of professional wrestling.

Marsh kept up the pressure on Curley's group by posting a $1,000 check with a Chicago newspaper. Marsh told the reporter in a story picked up by newspapers across the United States that Plestina offered the money for a winner-take-all match with Earl Caddock, Joe Stecher, Ed "Strangler" Lewis, or Charley Cutler.[xlv]

While the check did not tempt three of the Big Four, Charley Cutler could not resist the offer. Cutler agreed to wrestle Plestina in December 1917. Plestina wrestled Cutler in an inconclusive two-hour, twenty minutes match. The referee awarded Plestina the match after a frustrated Cutler punched Plestina to bring an end to the debacle.[xlvi]

Promoters told the Kansas City newspapers that Earl Caddock may defend his world title against Plestina on the first card of the new year in January 1918. Like all the other matches with the "Big Four," the match fell through.

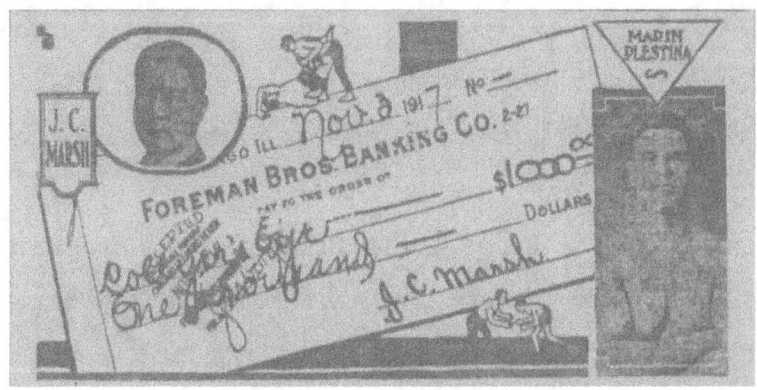

Figure 14 - Copy of Check J.C. Marsh deposited with a Chicago newspaper to secure a match against three of the Big Four and Charley Cutler (Public Domain)

Instead, Plestina wrestled Steve Savage in Detroit, Michigan on Sunday, January 27, 1918. Plestina won the match in two straight falls.

Cora Livingston, the Women's World Champion, also won her match in two straight falls. Despite Ms. Livingston's superior ability, the 1,000 fans booed the match as the fans came to see Plestina wrestle.[xlvii]

After the Savage match, Plestina traveled to New York City to issue a challenge directly to Jack Curley. However, Curley ignored Plestina. New York newspapers carried only short blurbs about Plestina's trip, a clear disappointment to Plestina and Marsh.

In early February 1918, Dr. Benjamin F. Roller agreed to wrestle Plestina. Detroit promoter James Howard also tried to book Plestina in a rematch with Charley Cutler. However, Cutler flatly refused to wrestle with Plestina again.[xlviii]

Cutler was smarting from his frustrating match with Plestina in Chicago. While Cutler's refusal pleased Jack Curley, Cutler's own irritation stopped the rematch.

The 42-year-old Roller wrestled the 30-year-old Plestina on Sunday, February 10, 1918. Fans considered Roller one of the all-time greats. However, Roller was on the downside of his legendary career.

Plestina applied a wristlock and arm scissors pinning Dr. Roller at thirty-six minutes of the first fall. Plestina pinned Roller with the same hold for the second fall and match at twelve minutes.[xlix] Plestina humbled Roller by using Roller's pet hold combination to pin the legendary Dr. Roller.

Plestina's victory over Roller cemented Plestina as a world title contender with wrestling fans. Plestina had a harder time convincing Jack Curley.

Meanwhile, Marsh secured a match for Plestina with Ad Santel in Chicago, Illinois on February 26, 1918. Plestina lived in Chicago and often wrestled on the Chicago cards.

Up until the day of the card, Chicago promoters advertised the match on a card with both Joe Stecher and Wladek Zbyszko wrestling different opponents. However, promoters substituted an opponent for Plestina at the last minute.

Chicago promoters never explained the sudden substitution. It is reasonable to believe Curley would not let Plestina wrestle on a card with his wrestlers. Curley told the promoters to remove Plestina or lose the bookings of Joe Stecher and Wladek Zbyszko.

What really happened came out in the *San Francisco Examiner* a week later. Marsh said he offered Jack Curley $1,000 if Plestina could not throw Caddock or Wladek Zbyszko once in an hour and thirty minutes.

Instead of Zbyszko, Curley tried to slip in Santel under the same circumstances. When Marsh and Plestina arrived in Chicago, they discovered promoters matched Plestina against Santel.

Marsh said Santel was a superior defensive wrestler, far superior to Caddock and Zbyszko. Plestina already defeated Santel in May 1917, but it took Plestina three hours to defeat Santel.

Marsh told the newspaper that Curley tried to slip Santel in to replace Zbyszko to hurt Plestina's reputation as a serious contender. Marsh told the Chicago promoters it was Zbyszko or Plestina was not wrestling. Curley did not give the promoters permission to book Zbyszko versus Plestina, so Curley forced the promoters to substitute another opponent for Plestina.[1]

Marsh and Plestina returned to New York to issue a challenge to the wrestling trust. Plestina offered to put up the $1,000 to wrestle both Zbyszko and Lewis in the same evening. Plestina told the New York newspapers they would donate the gate to World War I relief. Curley showed no interest in the challenge.

Plestina defeated both Hilmer Johnson and John Freeburg, while Plestina and Marsh were in New York. Despite Plestina's dominant two straight falls victories, Jack Curley continued to ignore Plestina.

Plestina's challenges nettled both Caddock and Stecher, who expressed a willingness to wrestle Plestina. However, Curley refused.

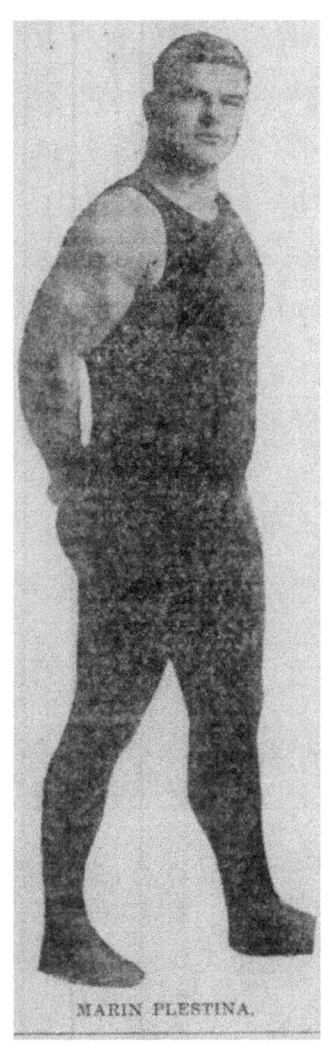

Figure 15 - Marin Plestina Circa 1918 (Public Domain)

Curley received help in combatting Plestina's claims in former World Heavyweight Boxing Champion "Gentleman"

Jim Corbett's weekly column. Corbett claimed fans and reporters did not take Plestina's claims seriously because Caddock defeated Plestina four years ago. Corbett also pointed to the controversial September 1917 match between Plestina and Joe Stecher as a reason not to take Plestina seriously.[li]

Promoters often planted favorable or unfavorable stories in newspapers in both professional boxing and wrestling. I cannot say Curley had anything to do with Corbett mentioning Plestina in his column though I would not be surprised. Joe Marsh also had friendly reporters who Marsh could turn to for positive coverage of Plestina.

Marsh announced in May 1918 that Plestina was taking a physical training instructor position with one of the Army camps around Washington, D.C. World War I tied up professional wrestlers in 1918 and 1919.

Unlike Jim Corbett, former light heavyweight champion Charley Olson endorsed Plestina as the best heavyweight wrestler in the game.[lii] The opinion of a respected champion further strengthened Plestina's call for a world title match.

On Tuesday, December 3, 1918, Marsh secured one of Plestina's few big matches during the years Plestina challenged the wrestling trust. Plestina wrestled a rematch with Charley Cutler in San Francisco, California.

Plestina wrestled Cutler at the Dreamland Pavilion in a two-out-of-three-falls match. Plestina won the first fall with a reverse head chancery and arm lock in one hour, eleven minutes, and thirty-two seconds. Plestina won the second fall and match in twenty-five minutes, twenty-three seconds with a head chancery.[liii] Plestina and Marsh struggled to book big matches with top name wrestlers.

Figure 16 -Taro Miyake in 1914 (Public Domain)

On Wednesday, December 18, 1918, Plestina closed out 1918 by wrestling a "jiu jitsu" contest with Taro Miyake in Vancouver, British Columbia, Canada. Plestina wore a judo Gi for the match contested under jiu jitsu rules. While we refer to this style as Japanese jujitsu today, it is noteworthy that most judo and jujitsu practitioners like Kosei Maeda, who taught Carlos Gracie, and Miyake wrote it as jiu jitsu.

The match drew a full house at Vancouver's Royal Theater with the audience being members of Vancouver's Japanese population.

The match was three twenty-minute rounds. If no one took a fall during the match, the referee Al Davenport would declare a draw. Sataro Fujita helped Davenport in interpreting the rules.[liv] Fujita taught judo in Vancouver starting around 1914.

Miyake tried for chokeholds while Plestina used his superior reach to hold Miyake off. Plestina applied a front face lock and took Miyake to the mat headfirst.

Plestina banged Miyake's head on the mat trying to soften Miyake up for the guillotine choke. Miyake resisted the tactic and kept Plestina from choking him.

Miyake threw Plestina five or six times but could not knock Plestina out or pin Plestina. By rule, neither Miyake nor Plestina could win the match with a perfect throw.[lv]

After one hour, Davenport declared the match a draw. Miyake never threatened Plestina, but Miyake was the first opponent to prevent Plestina from pinning him since Joe Stecher in September 1917.

It is amazing that Marin Plestina held out and publicly challenged the trust for four years. Jack Curley tried to force Plestina to fall in line by stopping Plestina from wrestling the top wrestlers at the time and enjoying the large gate receipts that such a match generated.

In early 1919, a new backer helped Plestina's and Marsch's cause. Bernarr

Macfadden, the owner, and publisher of *Physical Culture* magazine, publicly backed Plestina for up to $25,000 for a match with any of the "Big Four."[lvi]

Macfadden announced plans for a world title tournament during the first week of May 1919 in Madison Square Garden. Macfadden told the New York newspapers that if the Big Four refused to take part in tournament or agree to wrestle Plestina, Plestina would claim the World Heavyweight Wrestling Championship.

A self-made businessperson, Bernard Adolphus McFadden was born in Mill Spring, Missouri on August 16, 1868. An early proponent of physical culture, a combination of bodybuilding, gymnastics and sometimes boxing/wrestling, McFadden eventually changed his name to Bernarr Macfadden.

McFadden built a publishing empire focused first on physical culture before moving into pulp magazines like *True Detective*. McFadden used *Physical*

Culture magazine to promote Plestina and argue for Plestina's recognition as World Champion.

Dr. Benjamin Roller wrote for *Physical Culture* magazine. In a March 1919 article, Roller named Joe Stecher, Ed "Strangler" Lewis, and Marin Plestina as the best wrestlers in America. Roller also backed Plestina's and Marsch's claims that Jack Curley controlled the World Championship through the "wrestling trust."[lvii]

Despite Macfadden's backing, Plestina still struggled to find bookings. Plestina did claim the "real World Championship" since the Big Four did not show up for a tournament or agree to wrestle Plestina.

When Stanislaus Zbyszko returned to the United States in 1920, Plestina challenged Zbyszko, who accepted the match. However, Jack Curley canceled Stanislaus Zbyszko's bookings after Zbyszko accepted the Plestina match.

Stanislaus Zbyszko quickly backed out of the match with Plestina.[lviii]

Marsch expressed his frustration in a letter to the newspapers during April 1921. Marsch correctly predicted that Ed "Strangler" Lewis would drop the title to Stanislaus Zbyszko in May 1921.

Marsch also said the trust would end the 1920-1921 wrestling season the same way they did the year before by freezing Plestina out of the title picture. Marsch revealed that Stanislaus Zbyszko backed out on a $25,000 guarantee for the Plestina match. New York promoter Tex Rickard offered Zbyszko the $25,000 to wrestle Plestina.[lix] Curley forced Stanislaus Zbyszko to pass on the huge payday to get back in the trust's good graces.

As a reward, Curley arranged for Lewis to drop the World Heavyweight Wrestling Championship to Stanislaus Zbyszko for Zbyszko denying Rickard and Plestina the credibility that promoter and wrestler coveted. Zbyszko took the title, which he held for one year.

    Entering the summer of 1921, Jack Curley realized that he needed to end his promotional war with Tex Rickard. Curley could not ignore the challenge of the dangerous Plestina anymore. Curley had to choose the perfect wrestler to stand for his promotion in the legitimate contest with Marin Plestina.

Figure 17- Marin Plestina around 1917 (Public Domain)

Chapter 4 – Busting the Trust Buster

The roots of the feud between Tex Rickard and Jack Curley are still murky. Boxing historians claimed Rickard and Curley took part in a boxing promotion that lost Curley a significant sum of money. However, I cannot find a card where Rickard lost money. Rickard only made less of a profit than Rickard thought he would.

The only bout that could have caused the rift between Rickard and Curley was the December 1920 fight between Jack Dempsey and Bill Brennan. Dempsey fought this bout as a tune-up for the much-anticipated fight with Georges Carpentier, a French war hero.

Rickard paid Dempsey $100,000. Rickard paid Brennan $25,000 instead of the $35,000 that Brennan and Brennan's manager thought Rickard would pay them. After paying the fighters and expenses, Rickard paid $139,000 on a $145,000 gate.

Rickard profited only $6,000 on this fight.[lx]

Figure 18- Jack Curley circa 1910 (Public Domain)

Curley could also have been angry about the New York State Athletic Commission awarding Rickard exclusive rights to book Madison Square Garden. Right after losing the ability to book the Garden, the New York National Guard banned Curley from using the 71st Street Armory. Curley used the armory twice as much as he booked Madison Square Garden.[lxi]

Curley's standing with the New York State Athletic Commission reached an all-time low in early 1921. John R. Robinson, a newspaper reporter functioned as publicity press agent for the Jack Johnson-Jess Willard title fight in Havana, Cuba on April 5, 1915, wrote a series of articles about the fight in *Collyer's Eye*.

Jack Johnson provided the impetus for the newspaper series after leaving Leavenworth prison in early 1921. Johnson served a year for violation of the Mann Act. The federal government misused a law created to prevent interstate prostitution to charge Johnson, an African American, with a felony for having consensual relationships with white women.

A jury convicted Johnson in 1913 resulting in Johnson skipping bail and traveling to Europe. Johnson took the World Heavyweight Boxing Championship with him.

Figure 19 - Jack Johnson and his wife Lucille. The federal government first charged Johnson for transporting Lucille across state lines before they were married as a violation of the Mann Act. That prosecution fell apart. (Public Domain)

Johnson fought in England and France for the next two years. Eventually, United States diplomatic pressure forced both England and France to ban Johnson from boxing in either country. Neither country would deport Johnson back to the United States frustrating the American government's real goal.

With Johnson's main sources of income cut off and reports from America that Johnson's mother was ill, Johnson hoped to make a deal with the United States government for a reduced or suspended sentence.

Johnson knew the federal government would not listen to Johnson's request for a reduced sentence if Johnson still held the world title. Needing money and homesick, Curley found Johnson in the perfect position for Curley's business proposition. Curley offered Johnson $20,000 to drop the title to Willard.

Johnson agreed. Willard knocked Johnson out in the twenty-sixth round. The United States government did not agree to Johnson's offer to surrender for a reduced or suspended sentence, so Johnson took his large payday from the Willard fight and lived abroad until 1920. Johnson served his one-year sentence in 1920 and then exposed he and Curley fixing the Willard fight.

Curley denied Johnson's claims, but John R. Robinson wrote six or seven articles about the fight, Robinson's involvement in the fight, and the fact that Curley fixed the fight.

Editors at *Collyer's Eye*, a weekly newspaper dedicated to sports reporting with a focus on exposes, brought widespread attention to the fight fixing. *Collyer's Eye* also broke the White Sox World Series Scandal of 1919.

Robinson started the series on Saturday, February 5, 1921. Robinson authored an article for every Sunday edition until April 1921.

Robinson never names Jack Johnson's travelling companion other than to call him Young Cummins of Chicago. Cummins travelled with Johnson from Buenos Aires, Argentina to Havana. Johnson shared with Cummins his reasons for considering Curley's offer to take a dive.

Johnson told Cummins if he won the fight, he would only win the $30,000 purse and had no more legitimate fights in front of him.[lxii] Willard and Jim Moran were the only legitimate white heavyweights.

Johnson beat Moran in 1914. If Johnson beat Willard, Johnson would not be able to schedule another fight for three years. Johnson felt he would be too old to reach top shape for such a fight.

Johnson also told Cummins that if he beat Willard no one in America or Europe would buy the films of the fight. However, if Johnson lost, the fans of America, England, and France, who wanted to see a white man beat Johnson, would buy the films for an immense profit.[lxiii]

Johnson told Cummins he had decided to throw the fight but only if Jack Curley agreed to Johnson's terms. Johnson wanted $20,000, the film rights for the films sold to England and France, and Johnson's part of the gambling winnings for taking a dive.[lxiv]

Johnson met with Curley, and Curley's promotional partners Tom Jones and Harry Frazee at Camp Columbia outside of Havana. Curley agreed to Johnson's terms.

Johnson told the promoters that he would take a dive after the twentieth round of the forty-five-round fight. Johnson believed that athletic commissions would not question the outcome of the fight if Willard knocked Johnson out later in the fight.[lxv]

Johnson was right. Even after Johnson's admission and Robinson's articles with specific evidence of the scheme, a handful of officials and newspaper reporters still thought Willard defeated Johnson legitimately.

The New York State Athletic Commission did suspect Curley fixed the world title match. Even if Rickard wanted to partner with Curley, the athletic commission put every obstacle in front of Curley to keep him from promoting boxing or wrestling.

The Athletic Commissions actions forced Curley to work in the shadows. Curley booked his wrestlers with William Wellman, who controlled the Lexington Avenue Athletic Club. Curley and Wellman kept the agreement secret to prevent the New York State Athletic Commission from shutting down Wellman's operation.

Rickard secured the services of Marin Plestina, who was out of favor with the established promoters in 1921. Rickard signed Plestina to wrestle on Rickard's Madison Square Garden cards.

Rickard tried to pressure Curley into booking Curley's wrestlers with Plestina despite neither McFadden nor Marsch being able to force Curley's hand in four years of active campaigning. Plestina was attentive when Rickard approached Plestina about getting back at the trust promoters. Plestina thought a powerful promoter like Rickard may succeed where McFadden and Marsh failed.

Even though both Rickard and Curley loudly refused to collaborate with each other in public, both wily promoters knew the war was hurting both of their businesses. Rickard and Curley agreed to end the war in late 1921. Rickard had Plestina as his champion. Rickard and

Plestina figured Curley would pick Ed "Strangler" Lewis or Joe Stecher to stand for Curley in the contest to settle the war. Instead, Curley booked John "The Nebraska Tigerman" Pesek to wrestle Plestina.

Curley showed experience and cleverness by selecting Pesek as his representative. Lewis, Stecher, and Caddock all defeated Pesek in worked matches in the year prior to the November 1921 contest.

The public did not know the wrestlers worked the matches. If Pesek defeated Plestina, fans would no longer see Plestina as a challenger for Lewis, the current World Champion, or Stecher, the former World Champion.

Despite their public denials, insiders knew Rickard and Curley made a deal. Tex Rickard told newspaper reporters that Rickard would not work with Curley, even if Curley gave Rickard $10,000.[lxvi]

Figure 20- George Lewis "Tex" Rickard (Public Domain)

When Rickard flatly denied working with Curley, Louis De Casanova of the *Brooklyn Daily Eagle* approached Deputy

Commissioner Tom O'Rourke. O'Rourke acted for the New York State Athletic Commission at Madison Square Garden.

De Casanova told O'Rourke that Rickard not only signed Pesek, but Rickard also booked college and Olympic wrestler Nat Pendleton. De Casanova also said Ed "Strangler" Lewis and Stanislaus Zbyszko would wrestle at Madison Square Garden two weeks after the Plestina-Pesek match.

Rourke asked De Casanova if Rickard had made a deal with Curley? De Casanova said, "Not that you can tell." O'Rourke looked puzzled.[lxvii] O'Rourke knew that Curley would not allow Rickard to use Pendleton, Lewis, or Stanislaus Zbyszko to wrestle on Rickard's cards without an agreement of some kind.

When the wrestlers entered the Madison Square Garden ring on November 15, 1921, fans did not know that Pesek tried to cancel the match. Pesek told the officials that Pesek broke his arm in training. The commission's doctor checked Pesek's arm. The doctor told the commission that Pesek had a soft tissue injury, but Pesek could wrestle.[lxviii]

Plestina weighed 230 pounds, while Pesek weighed 184 pounds. The New York State Athletic Commission insisted that John Fleeson serve as referee for the match. The commission did not trust any other referee to officiate the match.[lxix]

The announcer told the crowd that the match was one fall with a two-hour time limit. Fleeson could order a third hour if neither wrestler scored a fall. However, the commissioners changed the format of the match after the first fall.

Fleeson started the match at 9:33 pm. Within five minutes, Pesek gouged Plestina's left eye. Pesek also head butted Plestina.

After five minutes, the fans booed loudly. The referee warned Pesek about his continuous fouling. Fleeson told Pesek, "If you butt again, out you go."[lxx] After eleven minutes, nineteen seconds of Pesek gouging and headbutting Plestina,

Fleeson disqualified Pesek.[lxxi] The disqualification should have ended the match.

As the fans booed and appeared ready to riot, the four state athletic commissioners, including former World Wrestling Champion William Muldoon, ordered the men "to wrestle all night until a wrestler scored a fall."[lxxii]

Fleeson reluctantly restarted the match after a five-minute intermission. Plestina continued to wrestle defensively. Plestina never secured a hold nor retaliated by fouling Pesek.

Pesek did not try for any holds but headbutted and palm struck Plestina. Pesek also gouged both of Plestina's eyes. After twenty minutes, the gouging closed Plestina's eyes, which were red and swollen.

Fleeson let the match go on longer than he wanted to because Fleeson knew the commissioners wanted a finish. After twenty-four minutes, four seconds,

Fleeson disqualified Pesek a second time.[lxxiii]

Fans furiously stormed out of the building before the commissioners convinced half of them to return. The commissioners ordered Fleeson to continue the match.

Fleeson started to leave ringside, but O'Rourke convinced Fleeson to continue the match. Fleeson started the match for a third time.

Plestina could not see by this time and was unable to defend himself. Pesek slapped Plestina, used his forearm to rake Plestina across the face, palm striking Plestina's nose, and shoulder butting Plestina's face. Fleeson allowed the farce to continue for seven minutes before disqualifying Pesek.

Commissioner William Muldoon walked up the ring steps to order the match to continue but Fleeson had enough. Fleeson jumped out of the ring and told Muldoon, "I'm through. What else can I do?"[lxxiv]

The fans, who came back for the third fall, surrounded the commissioners screaming all kinds of insults at them. O'Rourke looked helpless and asked the fans, "What else could we do?" Muldoon told the ring announcer to let the fans know the commission had banned Pesek from New York for life.[lxxv]

The commission also suspended J.C. Marsh, Plestina's manager, for reasons known only to them. The commission lifted Marsh's suspension a month later.

Pesek left the ring sneering at the fans. Pesek walked defiantly to the locker room and surprisingly the fans did not attack him. Ed "Strangler" Lewis was not so fortunate.

Lewis stood in the lobby defending Pesek before a large crowd pushed Lewis out of the lobby and knocked him into the street.[lxxvi] Only a crowd of disgruntled fans could achieve such a feat with Lewis.

Plestina needed a couple of months to recover after seeing an eye specialist.[lxxvii] Trust promoters did start booking Plestina again after the fiasco in the Garden.

Tex Rickard did not give up after this debacle, but Rickard would give in not long after the Pesek-Plestina match. Pesek achieved Curley's goal of removing Rickard as a competitor. In Pesek's next contest, Pesek would stand for the other side against Curley and one of Curley's wrestlers, who wrestled on the undercard of the Pesek-Plestina match.

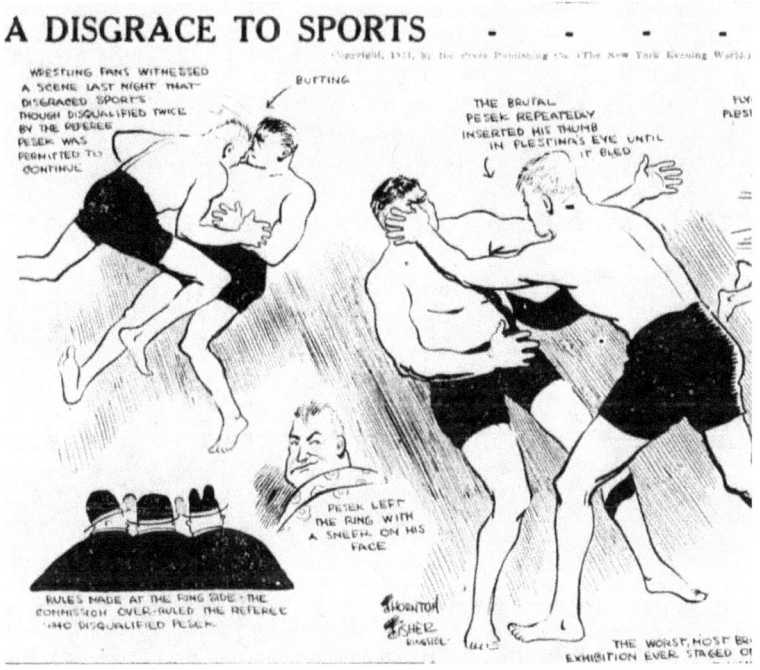

Figure 21- Artist Rendering of Pesek vs. Plestina in the New York Evening World (Public Domain)

Chapter 5 – Curley's New Challenger

Tex Rickard did promote the Stanislaus Zbyskzo vs. Ed "Strangler" Lewis rematch on November 28, 1921, at Madison Square Garden. Zbyszko won the rematch after losing the first fall to Lewis.[lxxviii] Ater this card, Rickard quietly stopped promoting professional wrestling.

With Rickard's withdrawal, Jack Curley won the promotional war. While Curley did not know it at the time, Curley would soon be in another promotional war. This time John Pesek would wrestle Curley's champion.

Jack Curley found a wrestler he thought would be a sure World Champion after the 1920 Olympic Games. Nat Pendleton wrestled for Columbia University and competed in the 1920 Olympic Games in Belgium.

Pendleton won two Eastern Intercollegiate Wrestling Association

(EIWA) championships in the years before the NCAA college championships in both 1914 and 1915.

Pendleton would have competed at the 1916 Olympic Games in Berlin, Germany but World War I forced the Olympic Committee to cancel the Olympics for the first time in its history.

Four years later, Pendleton wrestled for the United States in the 1920 Olympic Games in both Greco-Roman and catch-as-catch-can wrestling. Pendleton was not as familiar with Greco-Roman wrestling. Pendleton's lack of knowledge hurt him during the Greco-Roman wrestling tournament at the Antwerp, Belgium games.

Even though Pendleton competed in the heavyweight division in catch-as-catch-can wrestling, Pendleton wrestled in the light heavyweight division of the Greco-Roman wrestling competition. On August 18, 1920, Pendleton wrestled Johannes Eriksen of Denmark.

Pendleton had wrestled Eriksen for twenty-two minutes, when Pendleton put an armbar on Eriksen. The referee disqualified Pendleton for using an illegal hold.[lxxix] Eriksen went on to win the bronze medal in Greco-Roman wrestling.

Pendleton ran through everyone in catch-as-catch-can wrestling until Pendleton wrestled Robert Roth of Switzerland in the gold medal final.

The match went thirty minutes without a decision. The referee awarded the match and gold medal to Nat Pendleton. However, the judges reversed the referee's decision and awarded the gold medal to Roth. The United States Olympic Committee protested the unfair decision.[lxxx]

Experts at the Olympics agreed that Pendleton won the match. However, the decision stood, and the Olympic Committee awarded Pendleton the silver medal. Despite the official decision, Curley often claimed that Pendleton won the gold medal at the 1920 Olympics.

After the Olympics, Jack Curley approached Nat Pendleton about wrestling professionally. Curley succeeded in convincing Pendleton to make his professional debut on December 12, 1920.

Nat "The Panther" Pendleton wrestled Frank Yesco, a Swedish professional wrestler. Pendleton needed only nine minutes, thirty-three seconds to defeat Yesco with an arm scissors and wristlock at the 71st Armory in New York City.[lxxxi]

Curley lent Pendleton to Boston promoter George Touhey for Touhey's Christmas night wrestling extravaganza in Boston, Massachusetts. Pendleton defeated Henry Bernini in four minutes, fifty-one seconds.[lxxxii]

In January 1921, Pendleton told New York reporters what motivated him to wrestle professionally. Right after World War I, a recession contracted businesses around the world.

Figure 22- Nat Pendleton around January 1921 (Public Domain)

Pendleton worked for a New York company, Wyllis-Overland Company, as a salesperson. The economic downturn forced the company to let Pendleton go. Needing money for his wife and her brother, Pendleton accepted Curley's offer to wrestle professionally.[lxxxiii]

On Thursday, January 13, 1921, Pendleton was back in Boston for a George Touhey card. Pendleton defeated Tommy Draak, a professional wrestler from Holland, in two straight falls. Pendleton used the hammer lock to beat Draak in thirty-nine minutes, fifteen seconds, and nineteen minutes, respectively.[lxxxiv]

Pendleton headlined cards for Curley early in his career. In Pendleton's Brooklyn, New York debut, Pendleton defeated Harry Molish at the Star Theater. Pendleton used a head scissors and hammerlock to defeat Molish in twenty minutes.[lxxxv]

On Monday, January 24, 1921, Pendleton wrestled Alex Hedlund at the 71st Regiment Armory on the undercard of the Ed "Strangler" Lewis versus Earl Caddock world title match.

Pendleton defeated Hedlund in five minutes, ten seconds with a head and arm chancery.[lxxxvi] Pendleton ran through this early opponent who could not compete on Pendleton's level.

On Thursday, February 10, 1921, Pendleton wrestled John Fenfert at the Star Theater in Brooklyn, New York. Pendleton beat Fenfert in six minutes.[lxxxvii] Despite the quick victory, Pendleton played with Fenfert for three or four minutes before pinning him.

Pendleton wrestled his first name opponent at the end of February 1921. Curly matched Pendleton against the Original Masked Marvel, Mort Henderson. The 42-year-old Henderson was on the downside of a twenty-year career.

Henderson wrestled as a journeyman for his career before donning a mask in December 1915. The Masked Marvel gimmick saved the 1915 International Wrestling Tournament.[lxxxviii] The gimmick also set

Henderson up for the best pay days of his professional career.

Figure 23-Mort Henderson (Public Domain)

By the time Pendleton wrestled Henderson, Henderson was cashing in on his fame as the Masked Marvel to put over younger wrestlers as Henderson approached retirement.

Curley booked Pendleton against Henderson believing Pendleton would beat Henderson decisively. Curley planned to book Pendleton against former world champion Earl Caddock after Pendleton defeated Henderson.

Pendleton wrestled Henderson in the co-main event under the Stanislaus Zbyszko versus Charlie Peters match at the 71st Regiment Armory on Monday, February 28, 1921. Pendleton understood the importance of the match as Pendleton pressed Henderson for the entire match.

Pendleton almost defeated Henderson two to three times with a hammerlock. However, Henderson kept slipping Pendleton's pet hold.

Pendleton finally applied a head and knee chancery to pin Henderson at twenty minutes, forty seconds.[lxxxix] Curley announced that Pendleton would wrestle Earl Caddock next.

In an unexpected move on Curley's part, Curley tried to arrange a match between Pendleton and John "The Nebraska Tigerman" Pesek. Curley's signing of Pesek would lead to Pesek's brutal trashing of Marin Plestina that I covered in the last chapter.

Pendleton declined to wrestle Pesek. Pendleton preferred to wrestle Earl Caddock for the light heavyweight wrestling championship.[xc]

On Friday, April 22, 1921, Pendleton wrestled Ivan Padoubney on a training ship at the foot of 59th Street in New York City. Dr. Benjamin F. Roller refereed the main event match, which was the headliner of the event to raise money for a local charity.

Padoubney weighed 235 pounds to Pendleton's 190 pounds. Pendleton did not seem bothered by the weight advantage.

Padoubney wrestled defensively. Padoubney's tactics kept him safe for an hour. Pendleton chased Padoubney for the entirety of the match. Pendleton applied a hammerlock after about twenty minutes, but Padoubney slipped the hold.

Finally, Pendleton put a toehold on Padoubney, who kicked and bucked like mad. Pendleton stayed locked on the hold forcing Padoubney to give up after fifty-seven minutes.[xci]

After this match, Pendleton won a handful of matches against inferior competition until a lightly regarded challenger handed Pendleton his first setback. Karl Vogel, a 245-pound powerhouse succeeded in picking Pendleton up and slamming Pendleton.

Despite Pendleton's extensive wrestling experience, Pendleton made a newcomer mistake. Pendleton put his hand out to break his fall. The pressure on Pendleton's arm fractured Pendleton's clavicle.[xcii]

The referee should have awarded the decision to Vogel on a withdrawal. However, Vogel refused to accept a win because Pendleton could not continue. Vogel told the referee to declare the match a no decision.[xciii] Pendleton and Vogel embraced as Vogel helped Pendleton's seconds escort Pendleton back to the dressing room.

The injury sidelined Pendleton until November 1921. During Pendleton's recovery, Pendleton engaged in a verbal duel with members of the New York State Athletic Commission.

We already know that Jack Curley and Tex Rickard feuded during this time. Before Curley and Rickard could arrange a match, the New York State Athletic Commission enacted new rules for professional wrestling in New York. The commission banned four of the most popular moves in professional wrestling.

The New York State Athletic Commission banned the stranglehold, the headlock, the scissors hold, and the toe hold. While mayors, cities, and commissions banned the stranglehold since the days of Evan "The Strangler"

Lewis, commissions never banned the other three holds before the controversial NYSAC ruling.

While the banning of the scissors and toe hold did not make sense, the commission made an idiotic decision in banning the headlock. A wrestler using a headlock in a legitimate wrestling match is putting themselves in a horrible position. After taking their opponent to the ground, the wrestler is putting a skilled grappler on their back. While a handful of grapplers can keep an opponent locked in a scarf hold, most grapplers can escape and will be in a superior position.

Driving their decision, the commission fell for Ed "Strangler" Lewis's use of the headlock in wrestling matches. When Lewis was working to a finish, he threw his opponent three or four times with the headlock. After "softening" up his opponent, Lewis ground the headlock on the opponent until Lewis was able to pin the weakened opponent.

Lewis also carried a wooden dummy head, which he cut in half and put three giant springs between the head portions. Lewis squeezed the dummy to show how he practiced punishing his opponents. Except it was all for show.

Lewis never used a headlock in a legitimate contest. Lewis told his pupil, Lou Thesz, that Lewis did not even consider the headlock a legitimate hold.

While the commission's ruling infuriated Curley and Rickard, neither promoter publicly criticized the commission.

Nat Pendleton as a two-time National college wrestling champion and the 1920 Olympic Silver Medalist in catch-as-catch-can wrestling was the perfect spokesperson against the decision. Pendleton wrestled for Jack Curley. Pendleton was also friendly with Tex Rickard.

Pendleton told the New York City newspaper, "I see that the State Athletic Commission has revised the rules of wrestling and has barred the strangleholds, toeholds, scissors, and headlocks. If it were not for the fact that William Muldoon, the old-time wrestler, is head of the commission I should be strongly tempted to consider this action of the commission as a concerted effort upon professional wrestling to ruin its popularity in favor of boxing. It may be that Muldoon has not kept pace with the progress of wrestling in recent years. He is an old-time Greco-Roman wrestler and the so-called objectional holds were barred at that time."

"George Bothner, Dr. Roller, and all prominent wrestling authorities – even Marin Plestina – will bear me out that the prohibition of the headlock and scissors in their many variations and the toehold in moderation will do a great deal to destroy the spectacular value of the sport."

"I saw Tex Rickard yesterday morning and he told me that he is extremely doubtful now as to whether he would promote wrestling during the coming season due to the actions of the State Athletic Commission."[xciv]

Normally, the commission would fine a promoter or wrestler for criticizing them. However, the commission feared public backlash for acting against the popular Pendleton.

Fans loved Pendleton, who was a national hero after the controversial Olympics decision. The referee awarded the Olympic gold medal match to Pendleton, but the judges awarded the match to Pendleton's opponent. Newspaper coverage supported the referee and his decision.

The commission initially stuck to its ruling before quietly dropping the bans a couple of months later. The NYSAC never addressed Pendleton's comments.[xcv]

Pendleton spent the rest of his time off from wrestling preparing to return. Pendleton wrestled his first match after the injury in the co-feature of the John

Pesek versus Marin Plestina card. Neither man knew it at the time, but Pesek and Pendleton were on a collision course.

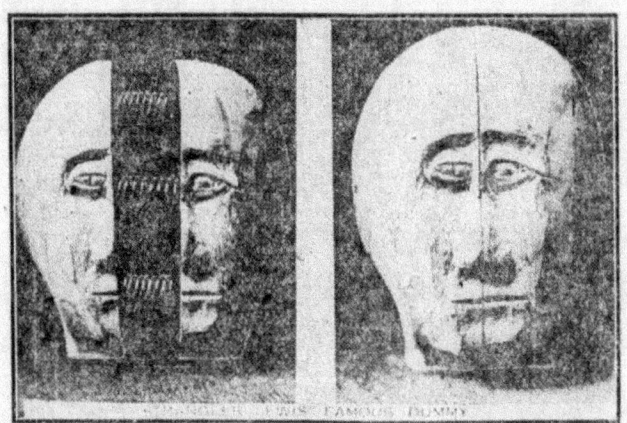

Figure 24- Ed "Strangler" Lewis's Training Dummy, which was a gimmick to help set up Lewis's headlock as a finishing maneuver. Lewis successfully fooled the boxing centric commissioners of the New York State Athletic Commission (Public Domain)

Chapter 6 – Pesek and Pendleton Before the Big Match

Nat Pendleton made a successful return to the wrestling ring on November 14, 1921, to wrestle "Chief" Newberry, a former Syracuse University Football player. Pendleton and Newberry wrestled a best two-out-of-three-falls match with a thirty-minute time limit.

Pendleton pinned Newberry for the first fall with a bar hold and reverse headlock in seventeen minutes, fifty-two seconds. Neither man scored another fall for the rest of time limit. The referee awarded Pendleton the match since Pendleton scored the only fall.[xcvi]

Curley started booking Pendleton into matches after Pendleton's victorious return. John "The Nebraska Tigerman" Pesek found himself in the opposite situation.

After the foul-ridden performance and the New York State Athletic

Commission barring Pesek from the state of New York for life, even Pesek's home state newspapers in Nebraska were calling for promoters to ban Pesek for life.

Figure 25- Artist rendering of the controversy (Public Domain)

Pesek's manager for the match, Larney Lichtenstein, placed the blame for Pesek's performance on Pesek. Pesek told a different story.

Lichtenstein, on orders from Curley, told Pesek to "gouge Plestina's eyes out." Lichtenstein told Pesek it did not matter whether Pesek won or not.

Curley wanted Pesek to permanently injure Plestina.[xcvii]

Lichtenstein denied Pesek's counter accusations, but circumstances favored Pesek. Larney Lichtenstein promoted boxing and managed boxers out of Chicago. Prior to managing Pesek, Lichtenstein did not manage wrestlers. Lichtenstein started managing wrestlers with Curley's help. After this controversy, Lichtenstein followed Rickard back into professional boxing.

While Pesek dealt with the aftermath of the Plestina match, Pendleton returned to the ring to wrestle Wladyslaw Bonecki. Pendleton wrestled Bonecki in the main event of a small event at the Rink Sporting Club in Brooklyn, New York on Thursday, December 1, 1921.

Bonecki had wrestled Frank Gotch in 1910. Bonecki lasted thirty minutes with America's greatest professional wrestler until Bonecki broke his ankle. The broken ankle forced Bonecki to withdraw from the match.[xcviii]

Pendleton wrestled with Bonecki for ten minutes before securing a half-Nelson. Pendleton forced one shoulder to the mat, but Bonecki used a head spin to stop Pendleton pinning him.

Pendleton switched to an arm and leg lock but struggled to move the two-hundred-pound Bonecki. Pendleton and Bonecki rolled on the mat for about two minutes before Pendleton pinned Bonecki.

The second fall was quick. Pendleton secured a head and arm scissors pinning Bonecki in thirty seconds. Pendleton pinned Bonecki twice in under fifteen minutes to the delight of Pendleton's hometown crowd.[xcix]

Pendleton still wanted to wrestle Earl Caddock to prove himself as a professional against one of the best wrestlers of the era. Caddock was not as eager to wrestle the up-and-coming young wrestler.

Pesek meanwhile was waiting for the outcome of his appeal to the New York State Athletic Commission for their lifetime ban. Pesek spent part of January helping his mentor, Clarence Eklund, train for a match with Pat McGill.^c

Figure 26 - John Pesek in 1921 (Public Domain)

To extricate himself from the New York situation, Larney Lichtenstein offered to sell Pesek's contract if someone made a lucrative enough offer. A group of New York investors offered Lichtenstein $20,000 for Pesek's contract. Lichtenstein said he would consider the offer.[ci]

Things were not all difficult for Pesek at the time. Pesek and his wife welcomed their first child on Christmas Eve 1921. Pesek admitted wanting a son but was overjoyed to welcome a beautiful baby girl into the family. The mention of his daughter brought a smile to the normally taciturn Pesek's face.[cii]

In late January 1922, Pesek appealed to the Nebraska Commission as well. Most state commissions followed the rulings of the New York State Athletic Commission. If other states accepted the NYSAC ruling, Pesek could only wrestle in states without an athletic commission severely limiting his options as a professional wrestler.

Frank G. Menke, the syndicated sports columnist, loved to put the screws to Jack Curley and expose the worked nature of professional wrestling. Menke had a source inside Curley's office because Menke often revealed information that only an insider could know. Menke accurately predicted Ed "Strangler" Lewis defeating Stanislaus Zbyszko for the world title in 1922.[ciii]

Menke revealed in February 1922 that Curley intended for Pesek to defeat Stanislaus Zbyszko for the world title in March 1922 instead of Ed "Strangler" Lewis. However, Curley changed his mind over the ham-handed actions of Pesek in Pesek's match with Marin Plestina.[civ]

Curley felt Pesek fouled Plestina so blatantly that Pesek brought unnecessary scrutiny to the trust. The NYSAC correctly assumed Curley gave the orders for Pesek to try to blind Plestina.

The New York State Athletic Commission ruling threatened to end Pesek's career if all the other commissions enforced the ban. Pesek put forth an odd defense in front of

Commissioner Lum Doyle and Secretary of Public Welfare H.H. Altes at his hearing on February 13, 1922, in Lincoln, Nebraska.

Pesek claimed that no one told him to deliberately injure Plestina. Pesek claimed Plestina fouled Pesek throughout the match. Despite Pesek's pleas to the referee, the referee did not penalize Plestina.

Pesek fouled Plestina out of frustration, but Pesek denied gouging Plestina's eyes. Commissioner Doyle expressed sympathy. However, Doyle also said that New York honored Nebraska's ban on boxers and wrestlers. If the NYSAC did not drop the ban on Pesek, Doyle said he would have to uphold the ban in Nebraska.[cv]

Jack Curley did try to persuade the New York State Athletic Commission to lift Pesek's ban. Unfortunately for Pesek, William Muldoon, one of the commissioners and former World Heavyweight Wrestling Champion from 1880 to 1889, feuded with Jack Curley throughout the 1920s.

Through political maneuvers, Muldoon denied Curley the ability to promote wrestling at the 71st Regiment Armory. Muldoon's actions forced Curley to book wrestling through promotional representatives.

Pesek faced a dire situation until an unlikely ally resurfaced. After initially blaming Larney Lichtenstein for the disastrous match, Pesek changed his story for the appeal hearing. Lichtenstein and Pesek shook hands. Lichtenstein agreed to manage Pesek still.

Lichtenstein lived and worked out of Chicago, where Lichstein exercised influence with the Chicago City Athletic Commission. While Lichtenstein worked to get a wrestling license for Pesek, Pesek mulled another friendly offer.

Jack Dempsey, the World Heavyweight Boxing Champion, was leaving on a trip for Europe. Dempsey invited Pesek to travel with Dempsey to Europe.

Dempsey also told the newspapers that Dempsey would put up $25,000 of his own money to secure a world title match for Pesek. Dempsey believed Pesek could beat any wrestler.[cvi]

Pesek made plans to leave for Europe with Dempsey, but Larney Lichtenstein delivered. The Chicago City Athletic Commission issued Pesek a wrestling license saving Pesek's career.[cvii]

The Chicago Commission issuing Pesek a license allowed other commissions to issue Pesek a wrestling license. Pesek wrestled throughout the Midwest as well as Boston, Massachusetts. However, the NYSAC did not drop its "lifetime" ban for seven years. Pesek returned to New York for the first time in early 1928.

Pesek did not wrestle big names in 1922 despite Lichtenstein's challenges to Ed "Strangler" Lewis with one notable exception. On Tuesday, May 16, 1922,

Pesek wrestled a rematch with Marin Plestina.

Plestina owned a forty-five-pound weight advantage over Pesek, who weighed 185 pounds. The promoters billed the match as one fall to a finish, but the athletic commission stopped the match after three hours, twenty-two minutes without a fall.[cviii]

Pesek wrestled aggressively for the first two hours, but Plestina's weight advantage started to wear on Pesek in the third hour. The referee Emil Thiery looked to the commission as both wrestlers showed signs of exhaustion. The commission halted the match to protect the health of the wrestlers.

Pesek did not foul throughout the match but did gouge Plestina's eyes at the fifteen-minute mark. Plestina showed reporters the scratches around his eyes after the match.[cix]

While Pesek did not hold a grudge with Plestina and worked with Plestina years after their match, Pesek did feel that Curley put Pesek's career in jeopardy. It would not take much effort from Billy Sandow to recruit Pesek for a legitimate contest with Nat Pendleton.

Figure 27 - Wladek Zbyszko in early 1920s (Public Domain)

Around the same time Pesek was fighting to continue his career, Pendleton continued building his professional reputation. In February and April 1922, an experienced wrestler handed Pendleton his first setback.

Incredibly, Jack Curley, Pendleton's promoter, caused the setback. An experienced promoter may be able to explain the booking of this series. As a historian, I cannot.

Curley booked Pendleton into a two-match series with Wladek Zbyszko, the "other Zbyszko." Based on accounts of the matches, Pendleton wrestled Zbyszko in legitimate contests. Zbyszko got the better of Pendleton in both matches.

In the first match, Pendleton wrestled Wladek Zbyszko on the undercard of the World Champion Stanislaus Zbyszko, Wladek's older brother, defending the championship against former champion Earl Caddock. Pendleton wrestled Wladek Zbyszko in front of 12,000 fans at Madison Square Garden on Monday, February 6,1922.[cx]

Zbyszko took Pendleton down to the mat at the start of the match. For the next twenty minutes, Zbyszko remained on top of Pendleton trying for the occasional hold but primarily just crushing Pendleton under his weight.

Despite his considerable amateur experience, Pendleton could not escape from the pressure of the 230-pound Zbyszko. Most writers attributed

Zbyszko's dominance to his forty-pound weight advantage.[cxi]

Still the result surprised mat observers. While Wladek Zbyszko owned a considerable professional experience advantage, the converted Greco-Roman wrestling specialist should not have been able to hold Pendleton down so easily.

If this result shocked followers of the sport, the rematch on Monday, April 24, 1922, at the Armory in Newark, New Jersey left onlookers speechless.

Pendleton wrestled a rematch with Wladek Zbyszko on the co-main event of the card featuring George Calza and Renato Gardini. Zbyszko again pinned Pendleton down for thirty minutes this time. Pendleton looked helpless as Zbyszko held him down for the entirety of the match. Zbyszko scored two to three near falls as well.[cxii]

The dominance of Wladek Zbyszko hurt Pendleton's growing reputation which brings into question why promoters booked the match in the first place. It is hard to see what Jack Curley hoped to gain by booking his budding star against a crafty veteran like Wladek Zbyszko.

Curley did use Wladek Zbyszko as a main event wrestler and world title contender. However, Curley was doing the same with Pendleton. While Curley would book Pendleton to lose to Zbyszko in the right situation, Curley would not want Pendleton to look so bad in the process.

Pendleton may have refused to work matches. If that is the case, I cannot see Curley booking the match between Pendleton and Zbyszko because Curley would not want to diminish the star power of his two biggest attractions.

If Curley wanted to teach Pendleton a lesson, Curley would have arranged a challenge training match in George Bothner's gym not in Madison Square Garden in front of 12,000 people.

Promoters only agreed to legitimate contests in front of the people when they needed to settle a promotional dispute and did not trust the parties to settle things in private. Promoters did not like legitimate contests not only because the promoter could not control the outcome. Fans often found legitimate contests boring. I do not see how this booking helped Jack Curley, Wladek Zbyszko, or Nat Pendleton.

Pendleton resumed his winning ways on Wednesday, May 17, 2024, in Englewood, New Jersey. Pendleton wrestled the "Great Massimo," who Physical Culture Magazine called the "world's most perfectly developed man."[cxiii]

Pendleton wrestled Massimo at Englewood's Armory in a two-out-of-three falls main event. While Massimo owned the impressive physique, Pendleton had the wrestling skills.

Pendleton came close to scoring an early quick fall with a body scissors. Massimo exerted powerful pressure on Pendleton's legs to escape the hold.

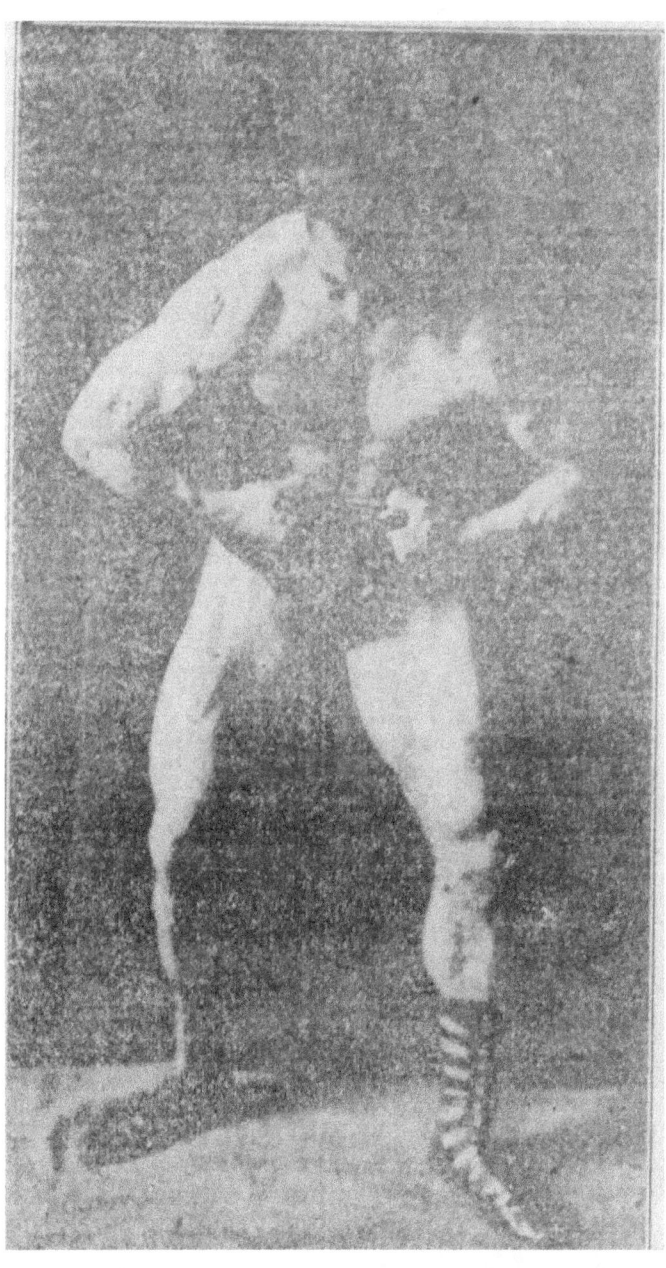

Figure 28 - The Great Massimo circa 1922 (Public Domain)

Pendleton kept applying holds to Massimo who managed to stay near the edge of the mat causing a break each time. Pendleton finally used a half-Nelson and crotch hold to pin Massimo in the center of the ring in seventeen minutes.[cxiv]

Pendleton continued pressuring Massimo during the second fall scoring two near falls. Massimo executed his only offense of the match with a headlock. Pendleton reversed the headlock into a cradle hold on Massimo. Pendleton pinned Massimo at twelve minutes of the second fall to take the match in two straight falls.[cxv]

The crowd cheered both men as they left the ring. Pendleton was back to his winning ways.

On Friday, June 9, 1922, Pendleton wrestled the 356-pound Pierre Le Collose at the Englewood Armory. Promoter Stuart Robson was promoting his last card of the season. Most promoters shut down during the summer due to the heat prior to widespread indoor air conditioning.

Unseasonably warm temperatures in early June hurt the attendance for this show. Le Collose had been wrestling a long time, too long. Le Collose did not put Pendleton in any danger during the entire match.

Pendleton pressed Le Collose until Pendleton was able to apply a double arm lock to pin Le Collose in eight minutes, fifty seconds.[cxvi]

At the start of the second fall, Le Collose opened a cut over Pendleton's left eye. The referee stopped the match for a minute, so the doctor could treat the cut.

Pendleton returned to the mat in a foul mood. Pendleton picked Le Collose up and dumped Le Collose over Pendleton's shoulder.

Le Collose struck the mat with a thud. Pendleton pinned the dazed Le Collose at only fifty seconds of the second fall. Pendleton dominated Le Collose showing his maturation as a professional.[cxvii]

Pendleton claimed "The Open Championship" after this match. While Pendleton's claim was spurious, no one had beaten Pendleton. Wladek Zbyszko only took Pendleton to draws.

Entering 1923, Jack Curley had two wrestling stars, Wladek Zbyszko and Nat Pendleton, who Curley was building for potential world title matches. Unfortunately for Curley, Curley had less power in 1923 than any other point in his career.

Figure 29 - Nat Pendleton training in 1922 (Public Domain)

Chapter 7 – Upsetting an Olympic Champion and Jack Curley

In 1923, the New York State Athletic Commission's attempt to clean up professional wrestling focused primarily on trying to drive Jack Curley out of wrestling promotion in New York. The commissions actions forced Curley to book New York City through intermediaries.

Since the mid-1910s, Curley enjoyed being the strongest promoter in the United States and the head of what newspapers referred to as "the wrestling trust." Curley controlled wrestling promotion in New York City, the largest city in the United States and a lucrative market.

Curley also had a pugnacious personality that made enemies easily. Curley fell out with business partners throughout his career. Curley was also morally flexible and involved in questionable deal after questionable deal.

Besides trying to fix the Johnson versus Willard fight discussed earlier in the book, Curley managed Georg Hackenschmidt for the second Hackenschmidt versus Gotch match on Labor Day 1911. Hackenschmidt, a gentleman known for his honesty, told newspapers after the match that Curley kept $30,000 of Hackenschmidt's $43,000 purse.

Hackenschmidt entered the match injured. Hackenschmidt wanted to withdraw from the match to preserve his reputation and his fan's bank accounts. Curley also announced that all bets were off to convince the injured Hackenschmidt to go on with the match.

Despite the announcement, Curley sent bookies out into the crowd. Curley told insiders over the years that he made another $30,000 from the match betting on Gotch. If we believe Curley's claims, Curley made $60,000, while his injured client took home $13,000.[cxviii]

In 1922, Curley decided to put the World Heavyweight Wrestling Championship back on Ed "Strangler" Lewis, after Stanislaus Zbyszko had been world champion for ten months. Curley's decision led to future headaches for Curley and his promotional partners.

Curley's top attraction in New York was Wladek Zbyszko. Curley wanted to book Wladek Zbyszko against Lewis for a series of world title matches. Eventually, Curley would tell Lewis to drop the title to Wladek Zbyszko. Lewis and his manager, Billy Sandow, had other plans.

Lewis despised Wladek Zbyszko going back to their first match in Detroit during 1914. After Zbyszko fouled Lewis a couple of times in a worked match, Lewis punched Zbyszko leading to an all-out brawl.

The Detroit Police had to separate the wrestlers and quell the ensuing riot. The fist fight caused fans of both men to start fighting among themselves.[cxix]

During his second title reign, Lewis refused to defend the world title against two wrestlers, Wladek Zbyszko and Joe

Stecher. Lewis and Stecher feuded over who was the best wrestler during the 1910s with Lewis eventually surpassing Stecher. It was professional rivalry with Stecher, but Lewis still refused to wrestle him after defeating Stanislaus Zbyszko in 1922.

Billy Sandow had also tired of Curley overseeing the world title. Once Lewis had the title, Sandow controlled the most prestigious prize in professional wrestling.

Since Lewis could defeat any wrestler in a contest, Sandow now exercised the control Curley once wielded. Sandow, Lewis, and Joseph "Toots" Mondt eventually formed the "Gold Dust Trio" promotional group. The Trio controlled American professional wrestling from 1922 to 1925. Sandow helped local promoters setup operations in most fair-sized Midwestern towns lessening Curley's influence over American professional wrestling.

When Nat Pendleton met John Pesek, Curley was at the low point of his promotional career. Curley's earlier promotional partner Bill Wellman sold his license to promote wrestling at the 71st Street Armory to Matt Zimmerman. Curley and Zimmerman struggled to bring fans to the armory to watch Zbyszko defeat lesser talent.

Figure 30 - Wladek Zbyszko circa 1923 (Public Domain)

Curley used Nat Pendleton on the New Jersey cards that Stuart Robson promoted for the Curley office. Pendleton moved to New Jersey in 1922 where Pendleton wrestled two to three times a month.

Curley was not trying to promote Pendleton for a title match yet. Curley did claim Pendleton could defeat any wrestler in the United States under two hundred pounds.

In early August 1922, Pendleton made surprising headlines outside the ring. New Jersey Police arrested Pendleton for assault on the business manager of the *Long Branch Daily Record*.

Pendleton asked to make a phone call at the newspaper office on Tuesday, August 1, 1922, which the business manager okayed. However, the business manager thought Pendleton took too long and told Pendleton to leave. An enraged Pendleton took Bryant B. Newcomb to the ground.[cxx]

People who knew Pendleton expressed shock as Pendleton usually was soft spoken and polite in his dealings with people.

In court on Thursday, August 3, 1922, the judge heard the whole story. Newcomb left certain facts out of his version.

Newcomb did tell Pendleton to leave but swore at Pendleton. When Pendleton said there was no reason for insults, Newcomb, obviously not a wrestling fan, put his fists up to fight Pendleton. Pendleton took Newcomb to the ground to stop Newcomb punching him.[cxxi]

An office assistant also tried to jump on Pendleton, but Pendleton sent him to the floor next to Newcomb. A newspaper reporter picked up a chair and started to bring it down on Pendleton's head.

Peter Jarvis, a fellow professional wrestler, and Pendleton's training partner grabbed the chair out of the reporter's hand. Jarvis threw the chair out the open door of the office, which attracted the attention of two police officers.

The police arrested the wrestlers for assault.[cxxii] After hearing what happened, the judge continued the case. Prosecutors quietly dropped the charges the following day.

While I thought Pesek settled a promotional war when he wrestled Pendleton, the match started the real animosity between Curley and Sandow. Curley never forgave someone getting the better of him in a business deal.

Billy Sandow's real name was William Baumann. His younger brother Max Baumann helped Sandow manage the Sandow promotion's wrestlers. Baumann was the manager of record for John Pesek, who Sandow recently signed to their promotional team.

Curley wired to George Touhey, the Boston promoter who Paul Bowser would soon replace, that Pendleton would wrestle any man willing to test his skills against the Olympian. Touhey wired Baumann to see if Max Baumann was interested in Pesek wrestling Pendleton.

Baumann eagerly agreed so Touhey sent a wire to Curley saying he secured a wrestler who weighed less than 190 pounds for Pendleton. Touhey also said a side bet of $1,000 would be necessary to secure the match. Touhey did not tell Curley the opponent was John "The Nebraska Tigerman" Pesek.[cxxiii]

Curley agreed but said the opponent needed to raise a side bet of $5,000. Baumann agreed and the match was set. Only then did George Touhey tell Jack Curley that Pendleton would wrestle Pesek.

Curley insisted that Pesek weigh in under 190 pounds. Pesek weighed in at 184 pounds forcing Curley to agree to the match.[cxxiv]

The *Boston Post* declared the Pesek-Pendleton match would be a "shoot" for a $7,000 purse. The match occurred at the Boston Grand Opera House on January 25, 1923. To win, Pesek had to pin Pendleton twice in 75 minutes. If Pendleton could avoid Pesek pinning him, Pendleton would win the match.

Pendleton entered the ring weighing 202 pounds. More than 3,000 fans showed up to watch the match between Pesek and Pendleton. "Cyclone" Burns was the referee for the contest.

Pesek set out at once to injure Pendleton, who wrestled defensively as he only needed to avoid Pesek pinning him to win. Pesek pushed Pendleton towards the ropes to start the match. After getting behind him, Pesek secured a double wrist lock. The double wrist lock can damage the elbow and shoulder joint, but Pendleton was able to escape the move. Pesek secured a second double wrist lock, but Pendleton pulled his arm away again.

Pesek used the threat of a takedown to spin to Pendleton's back. After a trip, which put Pendleton on his stomach, Pesek secured Frank Gotch's pet hold, the toe hold, on Pendleton's right leg at the 35-minute mark. Pendleton quickly gave up by yelling, "Stop. Stop." Pesek won the first fall in thirty-five minutes, twenty seconds.[cxxv]

The men resumed wrestling after the 10-minute intermission. Pesek picked Pendleton up and slammed Pendleton down on his side. The impact strained Pendleton's arm.

Pendleton was helpless to prevent Pesek from securing a second toehold. With barely 5 minutes passed, Pesek submitted Pendleton a second time.[cxxvi]

Pesek and Baumann received half of the gate receipts, a $2,000 purse plus Jack Curley's $5,000. Sandow's promotional group enjoyed a good laugh, but Jack Curley would not forget. Curley bided his time until he could exact revenge on Sandow.

Pesek did not seriously injure Pendleton, who wrestled Jack Sherry a week later. Pendleton wrestled for close to full-time for another year before leaving for Hollywood to act in silent films.

Pendleton found even more work when films transitioned to sound. While Pendleton wrestled part-time until the early 1930s, Pendleton focused on his acting career from 1924 on.

Pesek on the other hand still had more shooting to do. Despite being close friends with the world champion, Pesek went into business for himself in 1926 trying to take the world title in a famous double-cross.

Figure 31- Nat Pendleton showing his hammerlock (Public Domain)

Chapter 8 – Life Before the Double-Cross

John Pesek made Sandow's promotional team ecstatic with his defeat of Pendleton leading to Curley losing $5,000. Sandow rewarded Pesek by setting up a world title match with Ed "Strangler" Lewis.

Sandow first booked Pesek against Alan Eustace on February 26, 1923, in Wichita, Kansas. Sandow placed promoters in cities throughout the Midwest, which were often more lucrative than the large population centers.

By setting up these smaller Midwestern towns, Sandow pulled the power base of professional wrestling away from New York and Boston to Sandow and his team in the Midwest. Local promoters continued promoting professional wrestling into the territory era long after Sandow's promotional group ceased to exist.

Figure 32 - Alan Eustace circa 1922 (Public Domain)

Alan Eustace homesteaded or remained, in the Kansas territory, so he never achieved the national status of Lewis, Stecher, or Pesek. Eustace enjoyed a strong local reputation and wrestled the current world champion during the champion's tour of Kansas.

Sandow knew he could build a big card around Lewis versus Pesek, if Pesek defeated the name wrestlers around Kansas City, Missouri. Kansas City wrestling fans filled the Convention Center to watch the wrestling cards. Sandow and his promotional partners often drew crowds of 10,000 fans to see the local cards.

Pesek defeated Eustace in two straight falls to setup a title match with Lewis. Pesek took the first fall in 64 minutes. Pesek won the second fall and match in 42 minutes. Pesek used the leg scissors and armlock combination to win both falls.[cxxvii]

On Thursday, March 8, 1923, Pesek wrestled Joseph "Toots" Mondt at Kansas City's Convention Hall. The *Kansas City Times* reporter estimated the crowd to be between five and six thousand fans.[cxxviii]

In a lively worked match, Pesek and Mondt fell out of the ring two or three times. Mondt held Pesek off for a while, but Pesek scored the first fall after one hour, fifty minutes, and fifteen seconds. Pesek used his head scissors and bar arm combination to pin Mondt.

Pesek won the second fall quicker using the same hold combination to pin Mondt in twenty-nine minutes, forty-five seconds.[cxxix] Mondt put Pesek over to setup the title match with Ed Lewis.

Figure 33 - Joseph "Toots" Mondt (Public Domain)

In 1923, Mondt had recently joined the Sandow promotion, which would be known in later years as the Gold Dust Trio. Mondt revealed himself to be a promotional genius in his early years with Sandow's promotion. Mondt produced the promotional tactics to publicize upcoming matches. Mondt also sped up the action inside the ring.

In setting up challengers for Lewis, Mondt, a shooter and hooker on the level of Lewis, often put the challenger over to setup the title match. In this position, Mondt could also dispose of any shooters or hookers wanting to wrestle Lewis. If Mondt or Lewis suspected a potential double-cross, Mondt hurt the opponent in the first match making it easier for Lewis to dispose of the challenger in the world title match.

Lewis did not need the protection, but Billy Sandow lived in dread fear that someone would double-cross Lewis. Sandow should have exercised the same caution when he put the title on a pure performer, Wayne "Big" Munn.[cxxx]

On Thursday, April 12, 1923, Pesek met Stanislaus Zbyszko at the Kansas City Convention Center. 5,500 fans attended the card a disappointment to promoter Gabe Kaufman.[cxxxi]

Kaufman said promoters would want a world title match between Pesek and Ed "Strangler" Lewis at the Polo Grounds in

New York City. Kaufman must have forgotten Pesek's lifetime ban.

Figure 34- Ed "Strangler" Lewis and Stanislaus Zbyszko pre-match handshake circa 1921 (Public Domain)

If the crowd size disappointed Kaufman, the match disappointed fans. Pesek won the first fall in one hour with a double-arm wristlock and head scissors combination. Zbyszko appeared groggy from striking his head on the floor when

Zbyszko's feet went out from under him by the edge of the mat.

Zbyszko made it back to the ring but collapsed before the start of the second fall. The referee awarded the match to Pesek as Zbyszko's manager Jack Herman withdrew Zbyszko from the match.[cxxxii]

After the match, Zbyszko checked into a Kansas City hospital. Herman cancelled Zbyszko's next three appearances.

On Wednesday, April 25, 1923, Pesek travelled to Chicago to wrestle another match with Alan Eustace. Pesek pinned Eustace for the first fall and match with a double-arm wristlock and body scissors combination in fifty-three minutes, thirty seconds.[cxxxiii]

On Wednesday, May 2, 1923, Pesek challenged Ed "Strangler" Lewis for the World Heavyweight Wrestling Championship in front of 11,000 fans at Kansas City's Convention Hall. Kansas City fans proved again that promoters could count on them to fill the Convention Hall for the right match.[cxxxiv]

L.W. Shouse, the manager of the Convention Hall, estimated the gate to be $25,000.[cxxxv] In 2024 money, $25,000 is equivalent to $459,156.00.

The crowd politely applauded the champion, Lewis. In contrast, the fans gave Pesek a standing ovation.

Walter Bates served as the referee. Bates started the match which was mostly Lewis and Pesek in a collar-and-elbow tie-up, bulling each other around the ring. Lewis showed his strength by being the aggressor shoving Pesek around the ring.

Fans soon started hissing Lewis who was not cheating. Lewis was roughly handling their favorite which was enough for the crowd to give Lewis the raspberry.

Lewis took Pesek down two to three times, but each time Pesek escaped back to his feet. Pesek tried to apply his pet hold, the double-arm wristlock, two to three times. Twice Pesek looked to have the hold locked in, but Lewis shook Pesek off both times.cxxxvi

Even though Lewis and Pesek worked this match, Lewis did not trust Pesek. Lewis only tried to apply his headlock one time in the match. If Lewis used the headlock, he would be allowing Pesek on his back. Lewis never used the headlock when he did not trust his opponent.

Pesek lifted Lewis off the ground and tried to slam Lewis to his back. Lewis escaped and did not try another headlock.cxxxvii If Pesek tried to double-cross Lewis, Lewis sniffed it out quickly.

Lewis applied a toe hold at one hour, two minutes of the first fall forcing Pesek to give up. Pesek summoned Dr. B.L. Sulzbacher to examine his leg. The doctor told Pesek that Lewis did not injure his ankle. The doctor diagnosed a bruised shin from an inadvertent Lewis kick to the shin.cxxxviii

The examination delayed the start of the second fall to thirty minutes. Lewis needed only two minutes, thirty seconds to force Pesek to give up to a second toe hold.

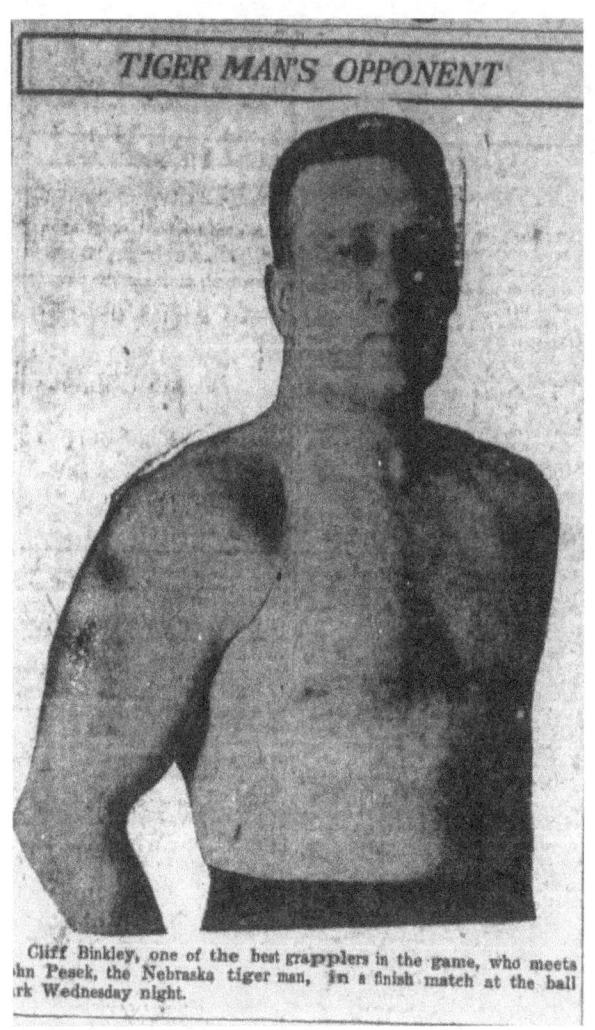

Figure 35- Cliff Binkley circa 1923 (Public Domain)

Pesek scored a major payday but his showing against Lewis turned off fans. The *Kansas City Times* reporter said Pesek needed to rebuild his reputation before fans would take Pesek seriously as a world title contender.[cxxxix]

Pesek returned to his winning ways in Nashville, Tennessee on Wednesday, May 23, 1923. Pesek wrestled well-thought of journeyman Cliff Binkley.

Pesek managed Binkley easily. Binkley outweighed Pesek by thirty pounds. The 184-pound Pesek picked up Binkley four- or five-times tossing Binkley to the mat.

On the last throw, Pesek followed Binkley to the mat and smothered Binkley. Pesek applied a double-arm wristlock and head scissors to pin Binkley at the thirty-five-minute mark.[cxl]

Pesek started the second fall by picking Binkley up and slamming Binkley into an awkward position. The slam accidentally or purposefully injured Binkley's shoulder. Binkley could not continue and gave up at five minutes of the second fall.[cxli]

Pesek took the summer of 1923 off but trained in his private gymnasium on his Ravenna, Nebraska farm. During July 1923, Pesek arranged a challenge match at his private gymnasium between his brother Charlie and Joe Stecher's training partner, Stanley Bures.

Figure 36- 1923 Star Automobile from the Public Domain

Charlie Pesek and Bures wrestled as middleweights or light heavyweights. Pesek bet $500 on Charlie while Stecher wagered a Star automobile. Charlie won the match. Elated over his brother's victory and winning the bet over Stecher, John let Charlie have the car.[cxlii]

John Pesek wrestled his first big match of the fall when Pesek wrestled Joseph "Toots" Mondt in Springfield, Missouri on Friday, September 29, 1923. The men wrestled in front of 3,000 fans at Springfield's Convention Hall.

Pesek and Mondt wrestled a two-hour draw. Billy Sandow's promotional group were using the match to build a world title match between Mondt and Ed "Strangler" Lewis.[cxliii] Fans did not know Lewis and Mondt were close friends and training partners.

Farming occupied more of John Pesek's time in 1924. Pesek wrestled infrequently in only big matches.

On Thursday, April 3, 1924, Pesek wrestled "Toots" Mondt in another match at Kansas City's Convention Hall. Pesek won the first fall of the two-out-of-three falls match at forty-nine minutes. Mondt won the next two falls and match in twenty-two minutes, fifty seconds and nine minutes, thirty seconds, respectively.[cxliv]

On Friday, June 6, 1924, Pesek wrestled Stanislaus Zbyszko in Duluth, Minnesota. 2,000 fans showed up to the auditorium. Zbyszko promised to throw Pesek twice in an hour or concede the match to Pesek. Pesek won the match, when Pesek threw Zbyszko for the only fall.[cxlv]

Pesek spent the rest of 1924 hosting shooting events on his farm as well as taking the occasional booking. This decision changed the business of professional wrestling and Pesek's wrestling career in ways Pesek could not have expected.

Figure 37- John Pesek in 1923 (Public Domain)

Chapter 9 – A Fateful Decision

The Sandow promotional group, led by Billy Sandow, spent 1924 building Wayne "Big" Munn into a world title contender. Munn played college football for the University of Nebraska. Sandow saw the potential to draw big money with the six-foot, five inch, 260-pound Munn.

By the end of 1924, Sandow decided it was time to put the world title on Munn. Sandow, World Champion Ed "Strangler" Lewis, and promotional genius Joseph "Toots" Mondt formed a promotional group known historically as the "Gold Dust Trio." The Trio drew a ridiculous amount of money from 1922 to 1925.

When Sandow told Lewis and Mondt about his plan to put the world title on Munn, both Lewis and Mondt told Sandow it was a terrible idea. Lewis and Mondt saw the money-making potential of the move. However, both Lewis and Mondt felt it was too big a risk to put the title on a pure performer like Munn.

Lewis and Mondt taught Munn how to work a plausible match, but Munn could not actually wrestle. Lewis told Sandow that a mediocre wrestler would defeat Munn in a legitimate contest. Mondt warned Sandow that anyone could double-cross Munn and take the world title.

Sandow assuaged Lewis and Mondt by promising to only book Munn against wrestlers loyal to and controlled by Sandow's promotional and management team. Lewis and Mondt reluctantly agreed to the arrangement.[cxlvi]

Lewis dropped the title to Munn in front of 10,000 fans at Kansas City's Convention Hall in January 1925. Lewis then travelled to Europe for a two-month tour.

In Lewis' absence, Mondt served as the primary protector for Munn. Mondt travelled with Munn to interfere in any attempted double-crosses.

The Sandow promotion also engaged Pesek to see off any challenges from other wrestlers, not controlled by Sandow, who came out to challenge Munn. The other wrestlers knew Munn could not wrestle legitimately. The wrestlers hoped to force Munn into a title defense where they could defeat Munn legitimately.

Sandow controlled both former world champion Stanislaus Zbyszko. Despite Zbyszko being in his mid-forties, Lewis felt Zbyszko was one of the only wrestlers who could defeat Lewis in a contest.

Sandow trusted Zbyszko. Sandow intended to have Zbyszko put Munn over in a couple of big matches proving Munn a legitimate champion. Newspaper reporters questioned Munn's true ability in stories right after Munn's title win.

With Zbyszko tied up with Munn, it fell to John Pesek to deal with the challenges. Pesek's preference for legitimate wrestling made Pesek the ideal candidate to see off the challengers.

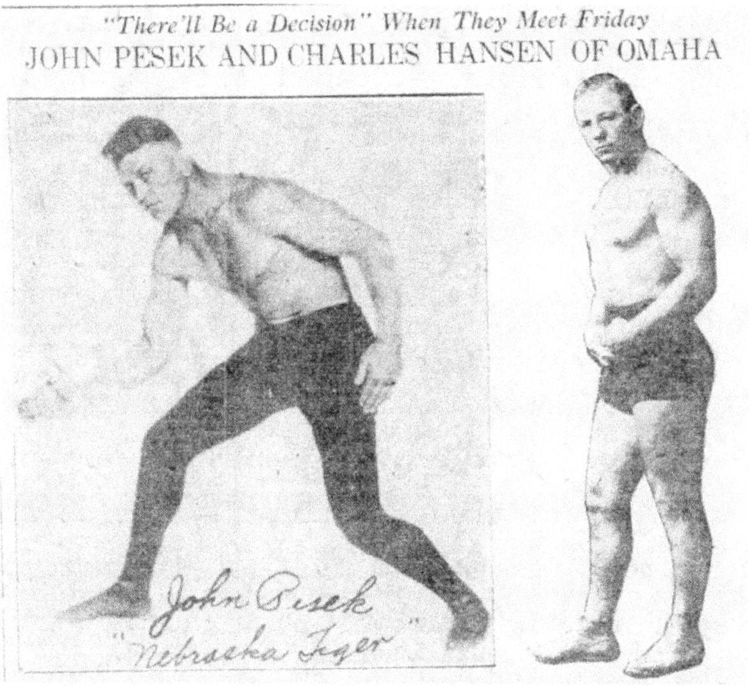

Figure 38- John Pesek and Charles Hansen from February 1925 (Public Domain)

Charles Hansen, an Omaha, Nebraska wrestler, loudly challenged Munn in January 1925. Hansen demanded a title shot. Sandow told Hansen that he needed to defeat Pesek to prove his viability as a contender.

Hansen ignored the demands at first but realized that Sandow would not give him a title match unless Hansen wrestled Pesek. Hansen agreed to wrestle Pesek in Hansen's hometown of Omaha, Nebraska.

4,500 fans attended the match at Omaha's Auditorium. Pesek wrestled Hansen in a best two-out-of-three-falls match.

Referee Paul Leidy started the match. It only took five minutes for Pesek to take Hansen down to the mat. Pesek applied a body scissors to Hansen.

Hansen struggled mightily but could not free himself from Pesek's steel grip. Pesek tried to adjust the hold which finally gave Hansen an escape route. Hansen flopped sideways and stood up.

Hansen thought he was free, but Pesek grabbed a leg and took Hansen back to the mat. Pesek applied another body scissors.

Hansen tried to rest and relax in hopes of tiring Pesek out. Seeing that Hansen was not going to give up to the hold, Pesek suddenly sprang away from

Hansen. Pesek and Hansen rolled back to their feet.

Pesek dumped Hansen back to the mat. This time Pesek applied a head scissors. Hansen tried to bridge. Pesek bore down on Hansen forcing Hansen's shoulders to the ground. Pesek won the first fall in twenty-six minutes, twenty-five seconds.[cxlvii]

After a twenty-minute intermission, Pesek and Hansen returned to restart the match. After the referee signaled to resume the match, Pesek took Hansen back to the mat.

Hansen stretched his feet out in front of his body and remained in a seated, defensive position for the next thirty minutes. Pesek almost secured a half-Nelson, but Hansen slipped it.

Hansen leaped to his feet. Pesek followed and dumped Hansen back to the mat. Pesek applied a second head scissors on Hansen.

Pesek squeezed his powerful legs around Hansen taking the remaining fight out of his fatiguing adversary. Hansen collapsed to the mat. Pesek won the second fall and match in thirty-seven minutes.[cxlviii]

Hansen's seconds carried Hansen from the ring. Pesek looked tired but walked back to the dressing room with his head held high. Pesek dispatched another "trust buster."

When Pesek returned to Ravenna after seeing off Hansen, 1,000 Ravenna citizens turned out to greet Pesek on his return from Omaha. Pesek stood on a baggage truck to accept the adulation of the crowd but refused to make a speech.[cxlix] Pesek preferred to let his actions speak for themselves.

Jack Curley had no qualms about making a speech of his own in March 1925. Curley offered a list of ten names who Curley said he would back for $10,000 that any of the ten wrestlers could throw "Big" Wayne Munn twice in thirty minutes. Curley complained that Munn was hiding behind Pesek.

Max Baumann, Pesek's manager and Billy Sandow's younger brother, responded to the newspapers. Baumann said Pesek was the only wrestler willing to wrestle anyone.

Baumann further said that Pesek agreed to throw Jim Londos and Vadelfi each in under ninety minutes in a winner take all match.

Pesek agreed to throw Daviscourt or Vadelfi five falls in an hour. Pesek also agreed to throw Joe Stecher in a winner-take-all match. Pesek posted deposits in Kansas City, Omaha, St. Louis, Chicago, Boston, and Wichita but the Stechers did not answer the challenge.

Pesek agreed to throw Gardini five falls in an hour. Pesek would then wrestle Londos, Stecher or Vadelfi.

After defeating all these foes, Pesek and Baumann would put up $25,000 for a match with Munn.[c1] This last statement was hyperbole as Sandow intended to put the title back on Lewis not Pesek.

Of course, everything Curley said was correct. The ten wrestlers could have beaten Munn. However, Joe Stecher was the only wrestler in Pesek's class.

Pesek and "Toots" Mondt would have spent the summer of 1925 seeing off challengers to Munn but the events of April 15, 1925, changed the face of professional wrestling for three years. Lewis's and Mondt's warning proved prophetic when Stanislaus Zbyszko, the wrestler Sandow trusted to protect Munn, double-crossed Munn in Philadelphia, Pennsylvania.

Zbyszko defeated Munn in two straight falls pulling off one of the most infamous double-crosses of all-time. Zbyszko dropped the title to Joe Stecher the following month.

Promoters had power with different athletic commissions, so Billy Sandow exerted his influence with a couple of commissions. The Illinois and Michigan Athletic Commissions refused to recognize Zbyszko's title win. Ed

"Strangler" Lewis defeated Munn in Michigan in May 1925 to claim the Illinois and Michigan versions of the world title.

The double-cross divided the world championship until Lewis and Stecher agreed to a contest in St. Louis in February 1928. The divided championship hurt wrestling at the box office forcing the two groups to settle their feud.[cli]

Pesek wrestled Frank Bruno on the under card of the Zbyszko-Munn match in Philadelphia. Pesek agreed to throw Bruno five times in an hour or give Bruno $2,000.

Pesek pinned Bruno for the first fall in seven minutes, forty-three seconds with a double-arm scissors hold. Pesek won the second fall with double-arm lock and body scissors.

Pesek won the third fall in nine minutes, fifty-three minutes with a hammerlock. Bruno gave up before Pesek broke his arm.

Pesek pinned Bruno with a reverse Nelson in eleven minutes, thirteen seconds. Pesek pinned Bruno for the fifth fall with a head scissors and armlock. Pesek won all five falls in thirty-nine minutes, twenty-one seconds.[clii]

Despite Pesek being in the building when Zbyszko double-crossed the Sandow promotion, Pesek did not get involved. Max Baumann tried to talk to Zbyszko, but Pesek remained in the locker room.

The divided championship turned out to be a good thing for Pesek when it provided him with another opportunity. Stecher fearing a double-cross from his own partners defended the title with wrestlers Stecher trusted. One of the wrestlers Stecher trusted was his fellow Nebraskan, John "The Nebraska Tigerman" Pesek.

Figure 38- The physically impressive Wayne "Big" Munn, whose lack of wrestling ability led to wrestling's most famous double-cross (Public Domain)

Chapter 10 – The 1926 Series of Matches with Joe Stecher

John Pesek left the Sandow promotion at the end of 1925, but Pesek remained on good terms with both Sandow's and the Stecher Brothers's promotional groups. The Stechers booked Joe Stecher against John Pesek in three matches during 1926.

The first match occurred at the St. Louis Coliseum on Thursday, April 29, 1926. Promoter Tom Packs had been trying to arrange a match between Stecher and Ed "Strangler" Lewis. However, the old enemies were struggling to come to an agreement. Stecher and Lewis would not agree to wrestle each other until February 1928 although Packs did secure the match for St. Louis.

Pesek stepped into the void eager to wrestle Stecher. Pesek and Stecher outlasted much of the 8,000 fans, who came to see the "Scissors Master" take on the "Tiger Man". The first fall came after 3 hours of hard wrestling.[cliii]

The match began at 10:10 p.m. on the evening of April 29th. Pesek wrestled defensively at first. It took Stecher 53-minutes to gain his first scissors hold on Pesek, but Pesek bounced around until Pesek freed himself from Stecher's legs.

In the next hour, Stecher was able to secure his hold two more times, but Pesek escaped the same way each time. Pesek was able to put a hammerlock on Stecher's arm and almost injured the champion before Stecher reversed out of the hold.

Finally, after 3 hours of wrestling, Pesek secured his wristlock, a legitimate submission hold, which Pesek worked in this match, forcing Stecher to give up. The men retired for a 20-minute rest. Both men were noticeably tired, when the match resumed.[cliv]

Stecher had the better of Pesek during the second fall ending the fall with a double wing lock. It is one of the few matches that Stecher secured a fall with a hold other than his scissors hold.

The men started wrestling again after a 20-minute rest. At the 40-minute mark, Stecher lifted Pesek off the ground, started to lose his balance and dropped Pesek out of the ring. Pesek struck his head and the impact knocked Pesek unconscious.

Pesek's seconds carried Pesek from ringside as referee Harry Sharpe raised Stecher's hand at 3:20 a.m. on Friday morning. Pesek suffered a concussion, at least that is what promoters wanted the fans to believe. Pesek went to the local hospital.[clv]

Despite the match being long and boring at first, Stecher and Pesek worked this match. Both wrestlers may have wrestled cautiously because either wrestler could try to double-cross the other one, but Pesek worked with Stecher increasing Stecher's trust level with Pesek.

Stecher and Pesek wrestled their second match in 1926 in Los Angeles, California at the Olympic Auditorium on Wednesday, August 25, 1926. Referee Tommy Travers started the match at 9:12 p.m. The men wrestled a one-fall with a two-hour time limit match.[clvi]

Stecher and Pesek shoved each other around for fifteen minutes before going to the mat for the first time. Stecher applied a leg scissors. Pesek shook it off by bouncing Stecher around.

As Pesek escaped the leg scissors, Pesek grabbed a toe hold. Stecher escaped the toe hold around 9:30 p.m.

The men pushed each other around for thirty minutes before Stecher applied another body scissors at 10:00 p.m. Pesek escaped again.

At 10:10 p.m., Pesek pushed Stecher to the mat. Stecher fell on top of the referee to the amusement of the fans.[clvii]

Stecher applied a series of leg scissors. Pesek bounced out of each hold.

Around 10:30 p.m., Pesek applied another toe hold. Stecher escaped the toe hold but Pesek transitioned to a body scissors and wristlock.

After Stecher escaped, both men were near the ropes. Stecher rushed Pesek causing both men to fall through the ropes. The collision did not injure either wrestler.[clviii]

Back inside the ring, Pesek applied a body scissors. Stecher escaped. Stecher applied a head scissors and wristlock. Pesek escaped by the ropes.

At 11:10 p.m., Stecher and Pesek applied head scissors on each other without effect on either man. Travers stopped the match at 11:12 p.m. declaring a draw after the end of the two-hour time limit.[clix] The draw setup a rematch for October 1926.

On Wednesday, October 6, 1926, Stecher wrestled Pesek for the third time in 1926. 10,000 fans filled the Olympic Auditorium in Los Angeles, California.

The Los Angeles match was following the same pattern as earlier bouts. Both Stecher and Pesek had won a fall. Stecher won the first fall in forty-one minutes with a double bar arm. Pesek won the second fall in twenty-one minutes, forty-five seconds with a head scissors and double-arm wristlock.[clx]

15 minutes into the third fall, Pesek applied a double-arm wristlock. Since Stecher and Pesek were working the match, Stecher let Pesek apply his pet hold.

Pesek locked the head scissors and double-arm wristlock on Stecher. This time Pesek cranked the hold on Stecher. Stecher and referee Tom Travers realized that Pesek was double-crossing Stecher.

Stecher had no choice but to give up to the armlock. Tom Travers ran around the ring trying to find a way out of the situation. Travers had no choice but to pat Pesek on the back to end the third fall at fifteen minutes, twenty seconds.[clxi]

Figure 40 - John Pesek circa 1926 (Public Domain)

The crowd started to stir as Stecher visibly wept in the ring. Tony Stecher escorted Joe to the corner and then spoke with Travers.

Travers shocked both wrestlers and the crowd though when Travers raised Joe Stecher's hand. While the announcer did not announce Travers decision in the ring, Travers told the newspapers the next day.

Travers ruled the head scissors to be an illegal choke. Travers awarded the third fall to Joe Stecher on a disqualification. Stecher was still the world champion.[clxii]

The crowd sat stunned for moments but as the decision sank in, they began throwing seat cushions and bottles at the ring. Police had to escort Travers out of the arena before the enraged crowd beat him unmercifully for the obvious bogus decision. Stecher and Pesek, both visibly shaken, returned to their dressing rooms.

If the situation had been a planned angle, it would have built to a huge rematch. Pesek's decision to shoot on Stecher prevented Pesek from gaining another title shot. The match also drew the attention of local authorities.

California State Athletic Commissioner Seth Strelinger held up the purses of both Pesek and Stecher. Strelinger summoned Pesek, Stecher, promoter Lou Daro, and referee Travers to Hollywood for a meeting to investigate the outcome of the match.[clxiii]

The *Los Angeles Evening Express* revealed the reason Pesek double-crossed Stecher. Pesek rejoined the Sandow promotion right before the third match with Stecher. Pesek intended to double-cross Stecher and embarrass Stecher at least but Pesek tried to take the title also.

Travers stuck to his story about why he disqualified Pesek. Promoter Lou Daro also said he saw Pesek dig his fingers into Stecher's throat. Daro said Travers had little choice but to disqualify Pesek.[clxiv]

The State Athletic Commission released the purses and let Travers' decision stand. Stecher defended his title for another year before agreeing to a legitimate contest with Ed "Strangler" Lewis in February 1928.

Pesek continued wrestling but he achieved greater fame in another arena. Pesek developed into the premier breeder of champion greyhound racing dogs.

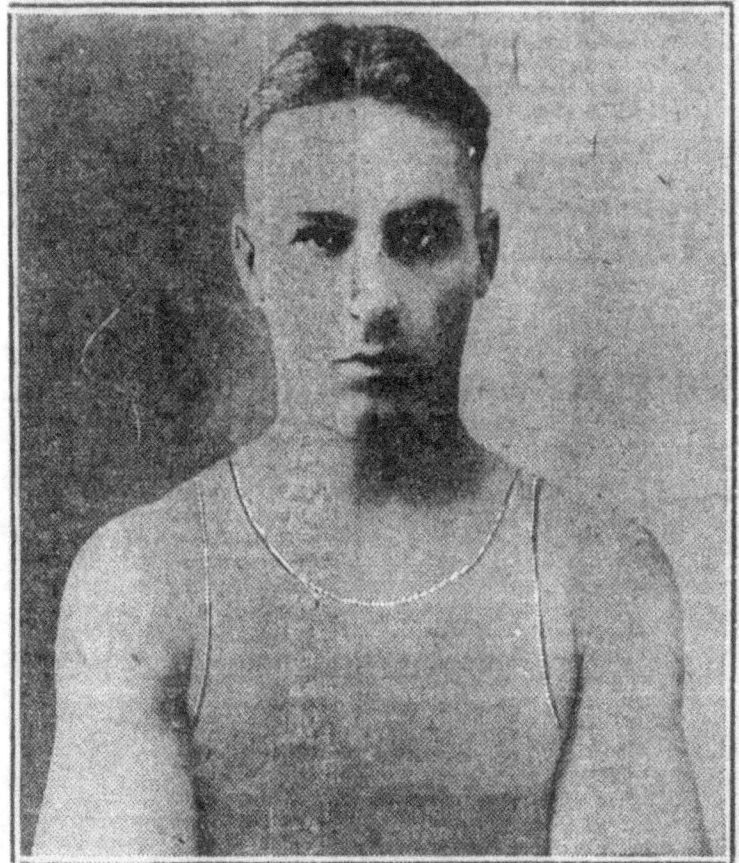

Figure 41- Joe Stecher in 1926 (Public Domain)

Chapter 11 – Champion Dog Breeder

John Pesek took part in greyhound racing from the early 1920s. In 1928, Pesek had fifty-six greyhound racing dogs on his Ravenna, Nebraska farm.

Pesek owned and ran the Rainbow Kennel Club from the farm. Pesek sometimes took the dogs to the racetrack. Other times, Pesek's brothers Charley and Hubert transported the dogs to the competitions.

On July 9, 1928, two of Pesek's dogs won races at the Highland Kennel Club in Anaconda, Montana. Pesek experienced success in greyhound racing but did not yet have one of the top clubs in the United States.

That changed in 1929, when Pesek travelled to Australia to wrestle a tour. The wrestling tour changed Pesek's fortunes in greyhound dog racing.

Pesek wrestled twenty matches during the Australian tour between July

1929 and November 1929. Pesek wrestled Allan Eustace, Ad Santel, and future world champion Jim Browning along with a handful of lesser-known wrestlers.[clxv]

Allan Eustace wrestled primarily in his home state of Kansas so Eustace travelling to Australia for a tour was unusual. Eustace was friendly with Pesek, which may account for promoters booking Eustace on this tour.

Ad Santel built a legendary reputation as a shooter and hooker. Santel defeated a handful of judo and jujitsu black belts in the 1910s in mixed styles challenge matches. Santel knocked out Taro Miyake in the second fall of their challenge match. Santel slammed Miyake to the mat causing Miyake to strike his head and knocking Miyake unconscious.

The 42-year-old Santel spent his later career putting over up-and-coming wrestlers while training them in shooting and hooking behind the scenes. Lou Thesz credited Santel with taking his legitimate wrestling skills to the next level in the late 1930s when Santel was in his fifties.

Jim Browning won the world title three years after this tour. Browning traveled to Australia to gain more experience. Browning also received help from Pesek and Santel on his legitimate wrestling skills. Promoters put the title on Browning during the era of the double-cross because Browning could protect himself and the title in a "shoot" or legitimate contest.

Pesek was still the bigger star, so Browning put Pesek over during this tour. Pesek won all his Australian matches, but Pesek's biggest victory was off the wrestling mats.

Toward the end of his tour in November, Pesek purchased two Australian champion greyhound racing dogs. The two dogs helped Pesek develop one of the top greyhound racing teams in the United States.

Pesek purchased Andy, an 82-pound greyhound, who won the South Wales Waterloo, the top greyhound race in Australia at the time. Australian greyhounds were larger than greyhounds in America and Europe. American and European greyhounds weighed between 60 and 65 pounds on average.

Keeper, the largest greyhound racing dog in America during the 1928 racing season, weighed seventy-four pounds. Pesek intended to breed Andy and Just Andrew, who weighed eighty pounds, with his greyhounds to make larger, faster racing dogs.[clxvi]

Fortunately for Pesek, he still had his brother Charles Pesek to help him with the greyhound stable. Promoters still wanted to book the nearly 40-year-old John Pesek, who knew he should take these opportunities as they would dry up as he aged.

Despite the widely held view that promoters feared booking Pesek after he double-crossed Joe Stecher in 1926, promoters not only booked him, but John Pesek won a version of the World Heavyweight Wrestling Championship on three separate occasions.

On Thursday, March 26, 1931, Pesek wrestled former opponent Marin Plestina from their infamous contest in New York ten years earlier. Since that contest, Pesek and Plestina worked four or five matches putting their bad blood behind them for the sake of making money.

Ohio promoters struggled to book current World Champion Gus Sonnenberg. Using a promotional tactic repeated by promoters throughout American wrestling history, the promoters created their own world title, the Midwest Wrestling Association (MWA) World Heavyweight Championship.

Promoters gave Sonnenberg a deadline to defend his championship against Pesek or give up the title to Pesek. Sonnenberg, a former professional football player and performer, knew Pesek would shoot on him and defeat Sonnenberg legitimately. Sonnenberg and his promoters ignored the ultimatum.

Once the deadline passed, the promoters booked the match between Pesek and Plestina for the MWA world title. The proliferation of world championships confused fans. Solving this problem was the impetus for the formation of the National Wrestling Alliance in 1948.

Pesek wrestled Plestina in Columbus, Ohio, in front of 7,500 fans in a best two-out-of-three-falls match with a two-hour time limit. Pesek won the only fall with a headlock and body pin in 79 minutes. The men wrestled the rest of the two-hour time limit without a fall.[clxvii]

The Midwest Wrestling Association awarded Pesek the world title based on Pesek's defeat of Plestina. Pesek defended the title for the next two years.

In early 1933, Pesek joined Jim Londos' promotional group. Since the Midwest Wrestling Association promoters did not work with Londos and his promotional group, the Association stripped Pesek of the MWA World Championship.

Outside of wrestling, an incident at John Pesek's farm on August 4, 1934, changed John Pesek's life and career. Charles Pesek, who was a year younger than John, acted on John's behalf in the greyhound breeding and racing business.

Always close, John convinced Charles to be his partner in the greyhound business, so John could continue his wrestling career. Charles proved as able as John in breeding and training greyhound racing dogs.

Under Charles management, the Pesek greyhound racing team won competitions around the United States. On the afternoon in question, Charles had just returned from a successful two-month racing season in Portland, Oregon.[clxviii]

Charles took cattle from John Pesek's farm to market to sell on the morning of Saturday, August 4, 2024. After selling the cattle at the government cattle sale in Pleasanton, Nebraska, Charles, and Melvin Pursell returned to John Pesek's farm. Pursell, a farm hand who travelled with Charles in Portland, was talking to Charles when Charles said he had been thinking about killing himself.

Pursell at first thought Charles was kidding but Charles pulled out a 38-caliber pistol. Pursell rushed Charles trying to prevent the tragedy, but Charles Pesek pulled the trigger. The soft nosed bullet made a grievous wound to Charles Pesek's head.

Charles Pesek lived until 4 a.m. on Sunday, August 5, 1934, at the Grand Island, Nebraska hospital, but doctors were unable to do anything to save Charles.[clxix] The tragedy left the Pesek family grieving with few answers about why Charles took his life.

Pursell said Charles appeared despondent on one or two occasions but did not give any sign that he was considering ending his life. Charles separated from his wife Pauline, but they separated two or three years earlier. Pesek's family did not think Charles Pesek would kill himself three years after his marriage soured.[clxx]

John Pesek lost his closest brother and his most trusted business partner. Pesek continued wrestling but stayed close to his Ravenna, Nebraska farm. Pesek wrestled in Lincoln, Nebraska and other Midwestern towns but did not venture farther than Ohio.

Pesek also focused on breeding the greyhounds and less on racing the dogs himself. Pesek's greyhound breeding operation made John Pesek a millionaire. Pesek never gave up professional wrestling but wrestled part-time and close to home for the rest of his career.

Figure 42- John Pesek and Just Andrew, a championship Australian greyhound that Pesek brought back to the United States in 1929 (Public Domain)

Conclusion

The New York Athletic Commission banned John Pesek from New York for life. The ban lasted for seven years, a short lifetime. Pesek wrestled throughout the United States in the 1920s. Entering the 1930s, Pesek wrestled closer to home to keep up with his burgeoning greyhound breeding and racing operation.

Prior to authoring this book, one of the myths I believed about Pesek was that after Pesek double-crossed Joe Stecher promoters stopped booking Pesek. However, facts do not bear out this version of history.

The Midwest Wrestling Association awarded Pesek the world title in 1931. The National Wrestling Association would also award Pesek the National Wrestling Association World Championship in 1937. The Midwest Association awarded Pesek their world title for the second and third times in 1938 and 1943.

Pesek wrestled until the mid-1950s when John Pesek was in his early sixties. Pesek wrestled into his later years to support his son Jack Pesek's professional wrestling career. John Pesek would make the occasional appearance to help promoters who booked his son.

I did not believe another myth about Pesek. In 1931, Pesek was supposed to wrestle a legitimate contest with Jim Londos. Years later, Pesek served as Londos' policeman to protect Londos from shooters and hookers. While Londos could shoot and hook, Londos never reached the level of hookers like Pesek, Ad Santel, Joe Stecher, or Ed "Strangler" Lewis.

Pesek got out of the contest by saying he fell off a horse on his ranch. Newspapers did report Pesek pulled out of the match because of a horse-riding accident on his farm.

Ed "Strangler" Lewis told Lou Thesz that Pesek did not like a straight up contest. Lewis said Pesek did not mind hurting guys who could not give him a problem, but Pesek backed off from real competition. Lewis felt Pesek feared an opponent beating Pesek in public.[clxxi]

Pesek's career dispels this myth. Pesek faced Wladek Zbyszko, Marin Plestina, and even Nat Pendleton in an underdog role. While Pesek surpassed Pendleton as a submission wrestler, Pesek would have a challenging time getting Pendleton in position for the submission. Pesek won all the matches except Plestina. Curley did not need Pesek to defeat Plestina. Curley needed Pesek to embarrass Plestina.

Pesek did not fear losing in public. Pesek could have hurt Londos. It was not a clever idea for Pesek to hurt the biggest box office wrestler of all-time. Pesek could make more money working with Londos instead of hurting Londos.

After retiring in 1957, the Nebraska Sports Hall of Fame inducted Pesek.[clxxii] Pesek continued to breed greyhounds. In 1966, Pesek lost his wife Myrl Pesek nee Mahoney with whom he raised three sons and four daughters.[clxxiii] Pesek outlived his wife by twelve years.

In 1973, the National Greyhound Association honored John Pesek as one of the all-time greats of greyhound racing. The Greyhound Hall of Fame in Abilene, Kansas enshrined both of Pesek's greyhounds Andy and Just Andrew as well as Pesek's champion greyhound Gangster. In the 1970s, 70 to 80 percent of the greyhound racing dogs in the United States descended from the two Australian greyhounds Andy and Just Andrew.[clxxiv]

On March 12, 1978, 84-year-old John Pesek had a heart attack and died at his farm. Heart disease did something that no wrestling opponent could ever do, keep John "The Nebraska Tigerman" Pesek down.

On Thursday, March 17, 1978, the Pesek family had John Pesek's funeral at Our Lady of Lourdes Catholic Church in Ravenna, Nebraska. Pesek's grandsons Bradley Pesek, John Pesek, Stuart Pesek, Greg Pesek, Jeff Pesek, Steve Nolda, James Van Herreweghe, and Sidney Van

Herreweghe carried their legendary grandfather to his final resting place in Highland Park Cemetery.[clxxv] Pesek was laid to rest next to his wife Myrl.

Because of his outside interests, John "The Nebraska Tigerman" Pesek did not achieve the fame of Ed "Strangler" Lewis, Stanislaus Zbyszko, or Joe Stecher. Pesek belongs in that vaunted company as one of the greatest legitimate wrestlers of all-time, who came along at the end of the legitimate wrestling era.

Figure 43- John "The Nebraska Tigerman" Pesek in his wrestling prime (Public Domain)

Other Combat Sports Books by Ken Zimmerman Jr.

Origins of a Legend: The Making of Ed "Strangler" Lewis

Wayfarer in a Foreign Land: Sorakichi Matsuda Wrestles in America

Shooting or Working? The History of the American Heavyweight Wrestling Championship

Gotch vs. Zbyszko: The Quest for Redemption

Double-Crossing the Gold Dust Trio: Stanislaus Zbyszko's Last Hurrah

Masked Marvel To The Rescue: The Gimmick That Saved the 1915 New York Wrestling Tournament

Gotch vs. Hackenschmidt: The Matches That Made and Destroyed Legitimate American Professional Wrestling

Evan "The Strangler" Lewis: The Most Feared Wrestler of the 19th Century

William Muldoon: The Solid Man Conquers Wrestling and Physical Culture

Morrissey vs. Poole: Politics, Prizefighting and the Murder of Bill the Butcher

Bibliography

Newspapers

Asbury Park Press (Asbury Park, New Jersey)

The Boston Post (Boston, Massachusetts)

The Brooklyn Citizen (Brooklyn, New York)

The Brooklyn Daily Eagle (Brooklyn, New York)

The Buffalo News (Buffalo, New York)

Collyer's Eye (Chicago, Illinois)

The Courier (Waterloo, Iowa)

The Daily Item (Lynn, Massachusetts)

The Daily News (Los Angeles, California)

The Daily News (New York, New York)

The Day (New London, Connecticut)

Des Moines Tribune (Des Moines, Iowa)

The Detroit Free Press (Detroit,

Michigan)

The Evening Daily World (New York, New York)

The Evening Standard (New York, New York)

The Evening World (New York, New York)

Evening World-Herald (Omaha, Nebraska)

The Fort Wayne Sentinel (Fort Wayne, Indiana)

The Gibbon Reporter (Gibbon, Nebraska)

The Grand Island Independent (Grand Island, Nebraska)

The Greeley Citizen (Greeley, Nebraska)

The Kansas City Times (Kansas City, Missouri)

The Kearney Morning Times (Kearney, Nebraska)

Kearney Semi-Weekly Hub (Kearney, Nebraska)

The Lincoln Star (Lincoln, Nebraska)

The Los Angeles Evening Express (Los Angeles, California)

Los Angeles Evening Post-Record (Los Angeles, California)

The Los Angeles Times (Los Angeles, California)

The Muscatine Journal (Muscatine, Iowa)

The Nashville Banner (Nashville, Tennessee)

New York Herald (New York, New York)

New York Times (New York, New York)

New York Tribune (New York, New York)

The Omaha Daily Bee (Omaha, Nebraska)

Omaha World-Herald (Omaha, Nebraska)

The Philadelphia Inquirer (Philadelphia, PA)

The Phonograph (St. Paul, Nebraska)

The Ravenna News (Ravenna, Nebraska)

The Record (Hackensack, New Jersey)

Reno Gazette-Journal (Reno, Nevada)

The Republican-Register (Aurora, Nebraska)

Rock Island Argus (Rock Island, Illinois)

St. Louis Globe-Democrat (St. Louis, Missouri)

St. Louis Post-Dispatch (St. Louis, Missouri)

San Francisco Bulletin (San Francisco, California)

The San Francisco Examiner (San Francisco, California)

The Shelton Clipper (Shelton, Nebraska)

Sioux City Journal (Sioux City, Iowa)

The Springfield News-Leader (Springfield, Missouri)

The Standard Union (Brooklyn, New York)

Star Weekly (Toronto, Ontario, Canada)

Times Union (New York City, New York)

Vancouver Daily World (Vancouver, British Columbia, Canada)

The Windsor Star (Windsor, Ontario, Canada)

The Zanesville Signal (Zanesville, Ohio)

Books

Gotch vs. Hackenschmidt: The Matches That Made and Destroyed Legitimate American Professional Wrestling by author.

Double-Crossing the Gold Dust Trio by author

Hooker by Lou Thesz

Masked Marvel to the Rescue: The Gimmick Which Saved the 1915 International Wrestling Tournament by author.

Origins of a Legend: The Making of Ed "Strangler" Lewis by author.

Websites

www.wrestlingdata.com

www.newspapers.com

About the Author

Ken Zimmerman Jr. is a married father and grandfather, who lives outside of St. Louis, Missouri. Ken has been interested in combat sports since watching professional wrestling from St. Louis in the late 1970s and his stepdad, Ernest

Charles Diaz, who raised him, introducing him to boxing. A lifelong martial artist, Ken holds rank in three martial arts including a 4th Degree black belt in Taekwondo.

If you like this book, you can sign up for Ken's newsletter to receive information about future book releases. You can sign up for the newsletter and receive a bonus e-book at www.kenzimmermanjr.com.

Endnotes

Chapter 1
[i] The Grand Island Independent, August 9, 1915, p. 2
[ii] Ibid
[iii] The Grand Island Independent, September 7, 1915, p. 2
[iv] The Grand Island Independent, November 1, 1915, p. 3
[v] The Grand Island Independent, November 24, 1915, p. 2
[vi] The Ravenna News, November 26, 1915, p. 1
[vii] The Grand Island Independent, December 15, 1915, p. 2
[viii] The Grand Island Independent, May 8, 1916, p. 3
[ix] The Grand Island Independent, May 24, 1916, p. 2
[x] Kearney Semi-Weekly Hub, July 24, 1916, p. 3
[xi] The Shelton Clipper, September 21, 1916, p. 1

Chapter 2
[xii] The Grand Island Independent, December 13, 1916, p. 2
[xiii] The Shelton Clipper, January 25, 1917, p. 1
[xiv] Wrestlingdata.com, Earl Caddock Record
[xv] The Kearney Morning Times, February 10, 1917, p. 1
[xvi] Ibid
[xvii] The Greeley Citizen, September 21, 1917, p. 1
[xviii] The Omaha Evening Bee, October 30, 1917, p. 8
[xix] The Grand Island Independent, March 30, 1918, p. 3
[xx] The Lincoln Star, October 21, 1918, p. 7
[xxi] The Ravenna News, December 13, 1918, p. 1
[xxii] The Republican-Register, March 26, 1919, p. 1
[xxiii] Ibid
[xxiv] The Ravenna News, April 4, 1919, p. 1
[xxv] The Lincoln Star, June 15, 1919, p. 7
[xxvi] Ibid
[xxvii] The Ravenna News, August 15, 1919, p. 1
[xxviii] Omaha Daily Bee, October 11, 1919, p. 17
[xxix] Ibid
[xxx] Ibid
[xxxi] Evening World-Herald, January 17, 1920, p. 5
[xxxii] Ibid
[xxxiii] Ibid

[xxxiv] Des Moines Tribune, December 29, 1920, p. 13
[xxxv] Ibid

Chapter 3
[xxxvi] Omaha World-Herald, September 4, 1917, p. 9
[xxxvii] Ibid
[xxxviii] Ibid
[xxxix] Ibid
[xl] The Detroit Free Press, October 30, 1917, p. 12
[xli] Ibid
[xlii] Sioux City Journal, March 13, 1910, p. 3
[xliii] Ibid
[xliv] Ibid
[xlv] The Courier, November 10, 1917, p. 14
[xlvi] Reno Gazette-Journal, December 18, 1917, p. 6
[xlvii] Detroit Free Press, January 28, 1918, p. 11
[xlviii] Detroit Free Press, February 4, 1918, p. 11
[xlix] The Windsor Star, February 11, 1918, p. 6
[l] The San Francisco Examiner, March 4, 1918, p. 12
[li] The Fort Wayne Sentinel, May 2, 1918, p. 12
[lii] The Buffalo Enquirer, July 10, 1918, p. 10
[liii] San Francisco Bulletin, December 4, 1918, p. 13
[liv] Vancouver Daily World, December 19, 1918, p. 12
[lv] Ibid
[lvi] New York Tribune, April 12, 1919, p. 21
[lvii] Ibid
[lviii] Double-Crossing the Gold Dust Trio by author
[lix] Collyer's Eye, April 23, 1921, p. 3

Chapter 4
[lx] The Evening World, December 17, 1920, p. 34
[lxi] The Brooklyn Daily Eagle, October 25, 1921, p. 20
[lxii] Collyer's Eye, March 19, 1921, p. 5
[lxiii] Ibid
[lxiv] Ibid
[lxv] Collyer's Eye, March 26, 1921, p. 5

[lxvi] The Brooklyn Daily Eagle, November 3, 1921, p. 14
[lxvii] Ibid
[lxviii] The Evening World, November 15, 1921, p. 22
[lxix] Ibid
[lxx] Ibid
[lxxi] Ibid
[lxxii] Ibid
[lxxiii] Ibid
[lxxiv] Ibid
[lxxv] Ibid
[lxxvi] Ibid
[lxxvii] New York Tribune, November 17, 1921, p. 15

Chapter 5
[lxxviii] Double-Crossing the Gold Dust Trio by author
[lxxix] New York Herald, August 19, 1920, p. 9
[lxxx] The Evening Standard, August 27, 1920, p. 1
[lxxxi] The Brooklyn Citizen, December 8, 1920, p. 8
[lxxxii] The Daily Item, December 27, 1920, p. 7
[lxxxiii] The Brooklyn Daily Eagle, January 11, 1921, p. 20
[lxxxiv] The Boston Post, January 14, 1921, p. 19
[lxxxv] The Brooklyn Daily Eagle, January 21, 1921, p. 24
[lxxxvi] Times Union, January 25, 1921, p. 8
[lxxxvii] The Brooklyn Daily Eagle, February 11, 1921, p. 22
[lxxxviii] Masked Marvel to the Rescue: The Gimmick Which Saved the 1915 International Wrestling Tournament by author.
[lxxxix] The New York Herald, March 1, 1921, p. 11
[xc] The Standard Union, March 8, 1921, p. 14
[xci] New York Herald, April 23, 1921, p. 10
[xcii] New York Tribune, July 14, 1921, p. 10
[xciii] Ibid
[xciv] The Brooklyn Daily Eagle, September 24, 1921, p. 12
[xcv] Ibid
[xcvi] The Daily News, November 15, 1921, p. 24

Chapter 6
[xcvii] The Lincoln Star, December 2, 1921, p. 14
[xcviii] The Brooklyn Daily Eagle, December 2, 1921, p. 26

[xcix] Ibid
[c] The Lincoln Star, January 15, 1922, p. 9
[ci] The Muscatine Journal, January 5, 1922, p. 9
[cii] Evening World-Herald, January 3, 1922, p. 10
[ciii] Double-Crossing the Gold Dust Trio by author
[civ] The Oakland Post Enquirer, February 3, 1922, p. 20
[cv] The Omaha Daily Bee, February 14, 1922, p. 8
[cvi] The Phonograph, March 1, 1922, p. 6
[cvii] Collyer's Eye, March 18, 1922, p. 4
[cviii] Rock Island Argus, May 17, 1922, p. 14
[cix] Ibid
[cx] The New York Times, February 7, 1922, p. 14
[cxi] Ibid
[cxii] The New York Times, April 25, 1922, p. 19
[cxiii] The Record, May 17, 1922, p. 8
[cxiv] Ibid
[cxv] Ibid
[cxvi] The Record, June 10, 1922, p. 8
[cxvii] Ibid

Chapter 7
[cxviii] Gotch vs. Hackenschmidt by author
[cxix] Origins of a Legend by author
[cxx] Asbury Park Press, August 3, 1922, p. 1
[cxxi] Ibid
[cxxii] Ibid
[cxxiii] The Buffalo News, January 31, 1922, p. 21
[cxxiv] Ibid
[cxxv] The Day, January 26, 1923, p. 13
[cxxvi] Ibid

Chapter 8
[cxxvii] The Kansas City Times, February 23, 1923, p. 8
[cxxviii] The Kansas City Times, March 9, 1923, p. 14
[cxxix] Ibid
[cxxx] Double-Crossing the Gold Dust Trio by author
[cxxxi] The Kansas City Star, April 13, 1923, p. 21
[cxxxii] Ibid

[cxxxiii] Chicago Tribune, April 26, 1923, p. 19
[cxxxiv] The Kansas City Times, May 2, 1923, p. 14
[cxxxv] Ibid
[cxxxvi] Ibid
[cxxxvii] Ibid
[cxxxviii] Ibid
[cxxxix] Ibid
[cxl] The Nashville Banner, May 24, 1923, p. 10
[cxli] Ibid
[cxlii] The Ravenna News, July 27, 1923, p. 1
[cxliii] The Springfield News-Leader, September 29, 1923, p. 5
[cxliv] The Kansas City Star, April 4, 1924, p. 20
[cxlv] Star Tribune, June 7, 1924, p. 29

Chapter 9
[cxlvi] Double-Crossing the Gold Dust Trio by author
[cxlvii] Omaha World-Herald, February 28, 1925, p. 21
[cxlviii] Ibid
[cxlix] The Ravenna News, March 6, 1925, p. 1
[cl] Star Weekly, March 21, 1925, p. 12
[cli] Double-Crossing the Gold Dust Trio by author
[clii] The Philadelphia Inquirer, April 16, 1925, p. 23

Chapter 10
[cliii] St. Louis Post-Dispatch, April 30, 1926, p. 44
[cliv] Ibid
[clv] Ibid
[clvi] The Daily News, August 26, 1926, p. 18
[clvii] Ibid
[clviii] Ibid
[clix] Ibid
[clx] The Los Angeles Times, October 7, 1926, p. 41
[clxi] The Daily News, October 7, 1926, p. 21
[clxii] Ibid
[clxiii] Los Angeles Evening Post-Record, October 7, 1926, p. 1
[clxiv] The Los Angles Evening Express, October 7, 1926, p. 27
[clxv] Wrestlingdata.com, John Pesek record
[clxvi] St. Louis Globe-Democrat, December 22, 1929, p. 46

[clxvii] The Zanesville Signal, March 27, 1931, p. 14
[clxviii] The Ravenna News, August 10, 1934, p. 1
[clxix] Ibid
[clxx] Ibid

Conclusion
[clxxi] Hooker by Lou Thesz
[clxxii] The Grand Island Independent, March 14, 1978, p. 2
[clxxiii] Omaha World-Herald, March 13, 1978, p. 11
[clxxiv] Ibid
[clxxv] The Grand Island Independent, March 18, 1978, p. 2

www.ingramcontent.com/pod-product-compliance
Lightning Source LLC
LaVergne TN
LVHW012017060526
838201LV00061B/4341